F*CKING AFFIRMATIONS

DAILY BADASS REMINDERS OF YOUR F*CKING GREATNESS

OLIVE MICHAELS

Sourcebooks, and the colophon are registered trademarks of Sourcebooks.

This publication is designed to provide accurate and authoritative information in regard to the subject matter covered. It is sold with the understanding that the publisher is not engaged in rendering legal, accounting, or other professional service. If legal advice or other expert assistance is required, the services of a competent professional person should be sought. —*From a Declaration of Principles Jointly Adopted by a Committee of the American Bar Association and a Committee of Publishers and Associations*

Published by Sourcebooks
P.O. Box 4410, Naperville, Illinois 60567-4410
(630) 961-3900
sourcebooks.com

Cataloging-in-Publication Data is on file with the Library of Congress.

Printed and bound in the United States of America.
VP 10 9 8 7 6 5 4 3 2 1

INTRODUCTION

Getting through the day-to-day while also remembering how badass you are can be an almost impossible task. Luckily, you have a collection of 365-daily reminders that you can read either in order or by flipping to any fucking page you want to get an awesome dose of inspiration and self-care. **No matter what challenges you face or what obstacles stand in your way, these affirmations will give you the courage to overcome them.**

On each page, you'll discover a new mantra that will help you embrace your inner strength and help you become the confident, empowered person you were always meant to be. Whether you're looking to boost your self-esteem, conquer your fears, or just need a little extra motivation to get through the day, F*cking Affirmations has got you covered.

So, what are you waiting for? Start living your best life, one swear at a time.

I MAKE A FUCKING DIFFERENCE IN THE WORLD

I'm here, I'm loud, and I'm not fucking going anywhere. Shout me down or tell me no all you want—I've heard it before—but I refuse to let anyone tell me I can't make a difference. I'm not afraid to take risks, not afraid of adversity, and I'm sure as hell not afraid to challenge the status quo. I make a difference by simply existing and doing my part to help create a better tomorrow. I'm passionate about making a positive impact, and I'm not afraid to stand up for what I believe in. I am constantly trying to make the world a better place in the ways that I can and the ways I know how—and I'm not afraid to fucking swear my way there.

I WON'T LET THE ASSHOLES BRING ME DOWN

I'm resilient and I won't let anyone deter me with their negative bullshit. I'm not going to give any anxious thoughts the time of day or any extra power. I'm here to squash that negative shit and remind myself that I have the power to be in control of my own thoughts and emotions. I'm not going to take any crap from anyone, and I'm sure as hell not going to let any crappy thoughts ruin my day. I'm going to stay positive and say, "Fuck you," to the intrusive anxious thoughts that come my way. So bring on the negative vibes, because I'm ready to obliterate them and be a powerful, badass woman!

I WILL OWN MY FUCKING SPACE

I'm not just a pebble in a pond; I'm the damn boulder right in the middle! I'm not going to let anything or anyone make me feel small. I'm strong and capable, and I'm not afraid to take up space. My voice is a force to be reckoned with, and I will not be silenced. I'm going to keep pushing forward and make sure my presence is known and respected. I'm a badass, and I'm not going to back down. I'm going to keep owning it and stay right in the middle of the pond.

I WILL BLOOM, BITCHES

I'm so fucking proud to be a woman and growing in all the ways I am. I know that gives me the power to create my own destiny. I'm learning valuable lessons from my own experiences and knowledge to grow stronger and wiser every day. I'm finally starting to embrace my own power, and I will continue to learn from myself, continuously evolving and becoming the best damn version of myself I can be. I'm ready to bloom—to take on anything that comes my way. This is my life, and I'm going to make it count.

I AM A FORCE TO BE FUCKING RECKONED WITH

No matter what life throws at me, I will confront it head-on and take no prisoners. I will not be defeated by my own negative thoughts or the low actions of others, and I will rise above and keep pushing forward, no matter how hard the challenge may be. I will take a deep breath and draw strength from my battles, knowing that I am superior to anything that threatens to bring me down. I will never give up; I will never give in. I am a fucking queen, and I will keep pushing forward.

I CAN AND I FUCKING WILL

Today, I'm saying yes to myself and fucking doing it. I'm a strong, badass woman who isn't afraid to take charge, and I'm going to get shit done. I'm not going to let piddly, inconsequential little shit like fear or doubt stand in my way, especially when I've got bigger and better things to do with my damned time. For better or worse, today I own my damn decisions. And no matter what happens, I'm sure as hell going to be proud of them.

I WON'T STOP UNTIL I'M PROUD AS HELL

I'm outrageously fucking proud of who I am and the things that I stand for. And no, I'm not afraid to let my voice be heard and to stand up for what I believe in. I won't let anyone dull my bad bitch sparkle or diminish my worth. I'm unashamedly me, I'm comfortable in my own skin, and if anyone has a problem with either of those things, they can kindly fuck off. I'll surround myself with people who respect and understand my values instead, and I'll live my life with passion and conviction. I'm at peace with myself, and I know what matters.

I'VE FUCKING GOT THIS

No longer will I let my worries and fears dictate my actions. I know that worrying is, before anything else, bullshit. It doesn't help solve any problems, doesn't move me forward, and will only create new ones. Instead, I vow that I will stay focused on the present moment and enjoy today to the fullest, embracing the here and now. I will not let any of my worries or doubts bring me down. I am a badass woman, and I will not let any amount of fuckery stand in my way. I will live and enjoy life to the fullest, without worrying about the future.

I. AM. KICK. ASS.

Being a badass means that I will learn to accept and embrace every part of me, both the good and the bad. I love other flawed people, and that means I have to love my own flawed self too. I'm not perfect, but that's just fucking fine. I'm going to be confident in who I am and celebrate all that I am, imperfections and all. I'm resilient and fucking amazing—and that's something to be proud of.

I'M FUCKING WORTH IT

I refuse to feel ashamed of my flaws and my perceived imperfections. I love myself and every single thing that makes me uniquely me. I'm learning to accept and embrace my mistakes and to be more compassionate with myself. I'm embracing all of me, the good and the bad, and I'm owning it like a fucking queen. I will learn to love my bullshit, my flawed self too, just like I love other flawed people. I'm fucking strong, and I'm fucking amazing.

I HAVE WHAT IT FUCKING TAKES

I swear that I have all I need in me to be successful as hell, and I'm fucking confident enough to make it happen. I'm not going to settle for anything less than over-the-top, mind-blowing excellence, and that's because I possess the knowledge, drive, and desire to fucking put in the work and make it happen. I'm not afraid to take risks and make bold moves. I'm going to fucking own every success and celebrate it to the fullest. I'm a damn powerhouse, and I'm going to make it happen, bitches!

I WILL BREATHE OUT THE BULLSHIT

I am so fucking done with worrying and stressing over what could be, what might happen, or what might not. My story doesn't have to be filled with fear and dread, and my day-to-day life sure as hell shouldn't be either. I'm going to take a deep breath, swear to myself that I'm motherfucking magnificent, and create a new story with a happier, more bitchin' ending. I won't let worry win—today or ever—because I'm a fucking champion, and I'm ready to take on whatever comes my way.

I'M NOT A DUMBASS FOR ASKING FOR HELP

You can bet your sweet ass I'm smart enough to recognize when I need help, and I'm not afraid to ask for it, either! I'm not a failure for needing support; I'm a badass for being brave enough to seek it out, and you can kick fucking rocks if you disagree. I'm proud of myself for understanding that I can't do it all alone and that it's okay to ask for help. I'm a powerful woman, and part of that power means taking a helping hand when I want or need one.

HELL YEAH, I AM IN CONTROL

I am a card-carrying, grade-A boss bitch, and you can be damned sure that I always have the power to choose a new path in life. I can choose to take risks. I can choose to play it safe. Both require courage in their own way, and I sure as hell am brave enough to make decisions that will ultimately lead me to success. I'm not just a passenger on this journey; I'm the fucking driver! I'm strong and competent, and I will never forget that I have the power to choose my destiny.

I WILL ONLY OWN MY OWN SHIT

Damn it, if I've said it once, I've said it a thousand times: I am not responsible for the actions of others. Everyone deserves the right to choose their own destiny, and I won't let myself be dragged down by the weight of someone else's karma. What other people reap they can damn well sow. I will focus on my own journey and not let the struggles of others affect me. I am not accountable for what anyone else is going through, and I sure as hell won't let myself feel guilty for something that isn't my fault or responsibility.

I WILL FUCKING CONQUER

Today, I'm going to stop procrastinating and take the fucking leap to do something I've been putting off. I know that I can achieve anything I set my mind to. I'm an accomplished motherfucker, and I'm going to use this day to make a fucking difference in my life. I'm ready to take on any challenge head-on, and I know I have the energy and skills to make my dreams a reality. So here goes nothing. Today I'm going to start making shit happen!

I WON'T SPEAK; I'LL FUCKING ROAR

Today I will channel courage and an undying self-love into my actions and behaviors. I am strong, powerful, and fuck-all determined, and I will not let anyone hinder me from achieving my goals. I will take pride in my accomplishments, and you can be damned sure I won't settle for anything less than I deserve. I will not let anyone make me feel small or unworthy, and I will speak up for what I believe in, and woe be to any dumb shit who tries to shut me up. I am a badass bitch, and I will make sure to always remember that.

I WILL MAKE TODAY MY BITCH

I'm taking some fucking control of my life, and I don't need to talk pretty to make it happen. I'm going to get shit done, and to hell with anyone or anything that stands in my way. All I need is a scorching hot cup of coffee, and I'll breathe fire over the obstacles in my path. I'm strong, capable, and I'm not afraid to get my hands dirty. I'm going to own today, and I'm not taking any shit. I'm on top of the things I need to do, and I'm going to kick ass. I'm ready to conquer the world, and I'm not afraid to do it with passion and fire. Let's do this.

FAILURE IS MY FUCKING FRIEND

I accept that some things won't always go my way. That being said, you can be damn sure that I will not let these moments define me. Instead, I will find peace and motherfucking serenity in knowing that I did everything I could, and move on. I have strength and resilience in spades, neither of which will never be reduced by any circumstance. And actually, I'll learn something from any obstacles or failures. No matter the day or the shit it may bring, I will keep my head held high and be proud of who I am and all that I have accomplished.

I AM READY AS FUCK TO MAKE MY MARK

I am done with settling for anything less than I deserve. I am ready to take control of my life and create the future that I want. I will surround myself with enthusiastic and motivated people who are determined to succeed and create a bright future for themselves. I will open myself up to the positivity and energy radiating from them and let it fill me with ambition and drive. I will kick ass and take names—and woe to the dumbass who tries to stand in my way. I will create a life I love, unstoppable in my faith in my own capabilities.

I WILL SHOW UP FOR MY DAMN SELF

I am overflowing with self-love and I'm fucking proud of it. I'm willing to do the hard work to make sure that I'm radiating that love into all aspects of my life. I'm not afraid to admit that I need help sometimes, and I'm committed to seeking out the resources and support that I need to make sure that I'm fully embodying that self-love. I'm independent as hell, but yeah, sometimes I need a motherfucking friend. Knowing that is its own kind of strength, and I'm going to use that strength to make damn sure that I'm showing up for myself in the best way I can.

THERE'S ONLY ONE ME, BITCHES

I will not let anyone else hold me back from being the un-fucking-believable woman I am. I am not here to be tamed, silenced, leashed, or restrained. I'm here to express myself freely, unapologetically, and fuck you very much if you have a problem with that. I will never let anyone else's judgment stop me from being and sharing who I fucking am, 100 percent honestly. I will continue to be true to myself no matter what tomorrow brings. This is my fucking life, and I'm not going to let anyone else tell me how to live it. This is me. And I'm proud of it.

I'M MY #1 FUCKING FAN

I am my biggest damn fan, and I'm also surrounded by people who believe in me and want to see me succeed. With their support and my own indomitable, bad bitch spirit, I'm unstoppable. My efforts are being supported by the most important people in my life—they are my cheerleaders, my fans, my fucking entourage, and they are pushing me to do amazing things. I'm grateful for their support, and I'm going to prove myself worthy of it by achieving all the things I set my damned beautiful mind to.

I WILL CELEBRATE MY DAMN WINS

I am fucking proud of all my accomplishments! I will use today to remind myself of my success and reflect on the recent wins I have worked my ass off for. No one can take away the hard work, dedication, and shit I have put in to make these achievements a reality. I am a fucking triumph and deserve to be celebrated for the wins I have earned. Today is another opportunity to remind myself of my greatness and to keep pushing forward. I got this!

I DESERVE MY OWN DAMN COMPASSION

I'm going to take care of me first today, no excuses. Fuck what everyone else thinks—I'm no longer going to allow anyone else's opinions to dictate my own self-care. Sure, it's unquestionably important to show compassion for others, but it's just as motherfucking important to show compassion for myself too. Just like everyone else I care about, I'm worth a bit of grace, patience, and self-love too. Today, I am going to prioritize that fact and focus on showing up for myself, no matter fucking what bullshit may come my way.

I WILL FEEL MY DAMN FEELINGS, THANKS

You can bet your ass that it's okay to feel scared, frustrated, and angry. To acknowledge my emotions means I'm strong and in control of my life. I'm more than capable of handling whatever comes my way, and I should never feel ashamed for expressing how I feel. Fuck anyone who tries to tell me otherwise. My feelings, fears, and worries are valid, and I'm fucking grateful to own them. Accepting that shit is the first step in managing my emotions, and that's exactly what I'm going to do.

I LOVE MY DAMN BODY

I am fucking rocking this life, body and all. I'm not ashamed of the person I am or the skin I'm in, and I'm not trying to change myself for anyone else. I'm confident in my own skin, and I'm fucking unapologetic about it. I'm not striving to become any other version of myself; I'm here, I'm alive, and I fucking love it. I'm grateful for my body, proud of it for all it has endured and all it does for me, and I'm going to continue to treasure it. I am who I am—and who I am is a fucking queen.

I AM FUCKING LOVELY

Yes, I am, and that is something I will remember to tell myself more often. Today, I vow to never forget that being kind and patient with myself is just as important as being kind and patient with others. Every time I look in the mirror or think about my talents, I can find something new I love about myself. I will sure as hell honor that love by being forgiving and understanding of my mistakes, just like I would be understanding of any other person I care about. All too often, this world will heap bullshit and fuckery on you for even the slightest mistakes—I don't need to add to that by doing its job for it.

I LOVE THIS FUCKING JOURNEY FOR ME

Damned fucking straight I can make mistakes and still be a strong, powerful woman. It's okay to not have all the answers—I'm busting my ass and learning every day, and that is something to be proud of. I'm forgiving myself for my missteps and embracing them as an integral part of my growth. I'm choosing to be gentle with myself, knowing that I'm still on the journey toward success. Understanding, after all, is fucking badass. I know that my mistakes are part of a beautiful journey—they don't define me but instead serve as a reminder that I'm growing and evolving into an even more killer version of myself.

I AM A RAY OF FUCKING SUNSHINE

Today I'm going to be radiant as hell and spread some positive vibes. I'm going to be a positive force for someone else—the most boss-bitch rainbow you've ever seen—and remind them that they deserve to be happy. I'm going to give them a reminder that they have the power to create the life they want. I'm not going to let anyone bring me down, and I'm going to give myself the same joy and respect that I give others. I deserve to be happy, and I'm sure as hell going to share that happiness with the people around me. I'll shine like a brilliant bitch and spread it around!

I WILL CLIMB; I CAN CONQUER

Fuck it. I am so beyond done worrying about the little things in life that I can't control. Instead of struggling to hold sand in my palms, I'm going to focus on what I can control—my reactions and my damn attitude. From now on, I will take an active stance on how I respond to the things that come my way and make sure that it's something that makes me proud. No more passively accepting outcomes, no more fixating on grains of sand when there are mountains to climb. I am meant for the fucking peak, and nothing will stop be from getting there.

I AM POWERFUL AS HELL

Today I will channel my inner strength and courage, and be a fucking badass. I will take on any challenge that comes my way, knowing that I am capable and powerful. I will be generous with my time and resources, spreading love and absolute buckets of fucking joy to others. I will be thankful for the opportunities I have and remain grateful for the amazing people in my life. I will embrace my femininity, and be proud of who I am and what I have accomplished. Today I will lace up my shit-kicking boots and let the world know I mean business.

I WILL DESIGN A LIFE I FUCKING LOVE

I am a powerful woman, and no one can stop me from achieving my dreams. I am the creator of my own destiny, and with hard work and dedication, I swear I can do anything. I have the courage, strength, and resilience to break through any barrier, any bullshit glass ceilings, and reach the top of the world. If anyone or anything stands in my way, too bad for them. They can pick up the pieces once I've shattered through them and left them the fuck behind, crying on the floor. Get behind me or get the fuck out of my way, because I'm not stopping.

I AM A SUPERNOVA OF BADASSERY

I will never let anyone or anything dim the badass light that burns within me. I swear on my fucking life that I will be my own lighthouse in the darkest of storms, my own guiding star in the night sky, my own light in the darkness. I will never be diminished by anyone or anything, and instead I will rise up and shine brighter than ever. I will be strong, I will be brave, and I will be unapologetic in my identity and my power. Nothing can take away my light, and I will continue to illuminate my own path, no matter what comes.

I WILL LEARN FROM MY DAMN PAST AND LIVE IN THE FUCKING PRESENT

I fucking swear to myself that I will not forget my past, no matter how much it hurts. I will not deny myself the opportunity to learn and grow from the mistakes I have made. Instead of telling myself to forgive and forget, I will remember to forgive and reflect. No more of this bullshit penance, no more beating myself up over the past. Instead, I will embrace the painful, precious fucking lessons that it has taught me. I have the power to recreate myself, and I will use those experiences to grow, let shit go, and become a better damn version of myself.

I WILL MOTHERFUCKING REAP WHAT I SOW

I refuse to be held back by anyone or anything. I will not allow anyone to take away my power or stop me from achieving my goals. I am strong and able to create the future I want for myself. I will never let fear, doubt, or negativity hold me back from realizing my dreams. I am the master of my own fate, and I am confident that I have the power to manifest my desired future. I will not be denied, and I will not give up. I am a warrior, and I will fight for what I want. This is my life, and I will live it to its fullest potential. The seeds of my success are within me, and I am ready to sow them and reap the rewards.

I WILL WORK THAT SHIT OUT

I am the fucking boss of my own future, and I will be damned if I let anyone tell me otherwise. Sure, sometimes self-care means doing the shit that might seem intimidating or overwhelming, but I'm doing it for my own damn sake and for the sake of my even more awesome future self. I can put in the work because I'm deserving of the absolute fucking best this life has to offer. And for all the asshats out there who question that? To hell with you; you aren't even worth a second of my precious fucking time.

I WILL NOT COMPARE MY SHIT TO OTHERS

Fuck comparison culture! I'm done with measuring my successes and failures against someone else's highlight reel. I won't let social media define me or the way I value myself, and that's fucking empowering. No more letting any bullshit external metrics define my worth. From here on out, I will keep showing up for myself. I'm taking control of my own damned life and focusing on my own journey, my own struggles, and my own accomplishments.
Nobody can take that away from me.

I AM GRATEFUL FOR MY FUCKING FRIENDS

Today, I'm going to prioritize my damn relationships. Whether it's sending a text to say hi to my mom or meeting up with an old pal for lunch, I'm going to make sure the people who matter most to me get the attention they fucking deserve. I commit to putting in the effort to connect with them and show them how much they mean to me. I'm not going to let all of life's bullshit get in the way of how important it is to build and maintain meaningful relationships. Here's to reaching out and expressing my motherfucking love!

I FUCKING TRUST MYSELF

Full stop. I believe that I have the power to make my wildest dreams come true, so long as I really fucking start believing in them. I'm done doubting myself—done second-guessing my abilities and ambitions. Instead, I'm now ready to unleash my true potential and work hard as a motherfucker to achieve whatever I set my mind and heart on. I'm not afraid to put in the effort, and I sure as hell won't let anyone or anything stop me from making my dreams a reality.

I WILL MAKE THE BEST DAMN DECISIONS FOR MYSELF

I am powerful and I have faith in myself to make smart, deliberate decisions in my life. I believe in myself and my capabilities, and I know that I'm sure as shit intelligent and capable of great things. I'm not afraid to swear and speak my mind because I trust my own judgment and intuition to guide me in the right direction. I'm an independent, strong woman and I won't let anyone or anything stand in the way of what I want to accomplish. I know I'm worth it, and I'm not afraid to do what it takes to get there.

MAXIMIZE GRATITUDE, GIVE BAD BITCH ATTITUDE

As I move through today, I will take the time to recognize and appreciate the wonderful person that I am. I will give gratitude to my body and mind, which work together in unison to guide me through life. I will embrace my strength, resilience, and capabilities, which make me fucking unstoppable. I will not allow anyone or anything to question my worth or minimize my accomplishments. I will be proud of who I am and remain confident in my capabilities. I will celebrate my successes and use my voice to stand up for what I believe in. I will own my power and never forget that I am a fierce, powerful, and incredible woman.

I AM EXACTLY WHERE
I NEED TO FUCKING BE

Hell fucking yes, I am present! Today, I will be mindful as fuck and optimistic too. I'll allow myself to let go of the unrealistic bullshit standards I've held myself to and the expectations of my future. Instead, I'm embracing the life that I'm living right now, in this moment, and recognizing that it is already a damn miracle. I'm ready to shape my own destiny and create the life I want and deserve, but that destiny starts today, and I won't lose sight of that. With each fucking second I spend in gratitude, I will ensure that nothing can stop me from achieving all that I can be.

I CAN TAKE THE DAMN RISK

Today I choose to look on the bright side and make the most of these twenty-four hours. I will pay attention to what's out there, and I will not be afraid to take some fucking risks if it means going after what I want. I'm going to kick ass and take names, and be proud of every single step I take like the badass I know I am. With a ferocious optimism and more nerve than even I know what to do with, I'll make my own damned decisions and forge a new path ahead, unafraid of the risk. Here's to the journey and, even more fucking importantly, here's to me.

I WILL MAKE COOL SHIT AND TAKE NO SHIT

Today is the day I take a stand and stop taking any bullshit. I'm the master of my own destiny, and I'm going to make choices that provide for my self-care, self-value, and self-worth. It's time to break any rules that don't serve me and create my own path—for my own success, for my own pleasure, for my own damn self. I'm done with feeling small and insignificant; today I move up and not back. I'm fierce, and I won't settle for anything less than I deserve. Fuck yes, let's get it done.

I AM FUCKING BRILLIANT

I've got a fire inside of me that's brighter than all the damn stars in the sky, and I refuse to let anyone dim my light, no matter how hard they try. I will find a way to be my own light in the darkness, and no one can fucking stop me from shining brighter than the sun and lighting my own path to victory. Rain may pour, snow may fall, clouds may come, but so long as I stay true to the inferno raging within this badass heart of mine, I will never be stopped.

I AM CONFIDENT AS HELL

Today I choose to take control of my own destiny and to refuse to let anyone or anything stand in my way. I will make the most of this day and every day to come. I will take the time to pay attention to the world around me, instead of letting it pass me by. I will not be hindered by negativity or let myself be dragged down by anyone else's bullshit. I'm a fierce, independent woman, and I will make sure my voice is heard. I am unapologetically me. Fuck the haters; I'm going to do me.

I BELIEVE IN MY DAMN SELF

I stand tall and empowered, fueled by the fire of ambition that roars within me. I am a powerful, dynamic woman, and I will not be diminished by the presence of doubt or hesitation. Asking for guidance is not a fucking sign of weakness or incompetence, but a sign of courage and determination. I am driven to succeed, and I am unafraid to seek guidance and advice when it is needed. I will not be held back or silenced by the naysayers; I will believe and fucking achieve; I know what I want and won't stop until I get it.

I WILL BE CALM AS FUCK

Today I will remember the moments that brought me peace this week and also recognize every fucking inch of progress I have made. I choose not to let the frustrations of the past keep me down, and instead I will push through them and focus on the peace and joy I have experienced. I am tough as fucking nails, and I know that I can take on anything that comes my way as long as I keep my head high and my eyes forward. I will not be deterred by the small shit, I will chill the fuck out, and I will stay true to my values and beliefs.

I WILL PAUSE BEFORE I BURN THE FUCK OUT

Fuck it, I'm not superhuman. I'm allowed to take a break and not be at my peak every day. I'm not going to be ashamed to say I need to rest and recharge—I sure as hell have earned it. Nobody's going to judge me for taking a breather and getting some much-needed downtime. And if they do? Fuck them. I'm going to do me and stay true to what my body is telling me. No fucking excuses—I'm going to treat myself with respect and make sure I get the downtime I need today.

I CAN POWER THROUGH THE CLUSTERFUCK

Women, I want you to swear this to yourself: I swear that I will not ever fucking give up. No matter what fuckery the world throws at me, I will stay strong and never surrender. I am capable of more than I could ever imagine, and I will never underestimate my power. I will make adjustments where I need to but never stop growing. I will revel in the challenge and never be afraid to be vulnerable. I will not allow anyone or anything to dull my shine. I will never give up, no matter what. I will keep going and keep fighting until I am victorious.

KNOWLEDGE IS POWER, AND I AM ONE KNOWLEDGEABLE MOTHERFUCKER

Today, I am overwhelmingly grateful for the lessons that life has to teach me. Every day is an opportunity to learn something new and discover more about our vast world—a gift that I sure as hell don't take lightly! With this in mind, I stand proud as a badass who embraces knowledge with open arms and an open fucking heart. It may not always be easy, but it makes me strong enough to tackle any challenge thrown my way. So this is my vow to myself: I will keep learning and growing each and every fucking day, knowing that these lessons are the best part of life!

I DESERVE A MEDAL IN BADASSERY

Today I'm embracing my awesomeness and all the effort it takes to be a badass woman. As I move through today, I'm taking the time to appreciate my body and mind for the amazing things they do to guide me through life. I know I'll make mistakes, but I'm also confident that I will learn and grow from them. I'm damn proud of my accomplishments and all that I have achieved, and I accept myself and my journey with love and admiration.

I AM MINDFUL AS FUCK

I am fucking grateful and I refuse to forget it. I will take a moment to look around and appreciate the beauty that surrounds me, as well as embrace my own. I'll rock my favorite ensemble, get some fresh-cut blooms, and make my favorite meal—anything to celebrate the incredible gifts life has given me. I'm a badass bitch, and I deserve to recognize my worth as well as the value of the awesome fucking life I'm building for myself. I'm here and I'm ready to fucking shine.

I WILL PUT THE PEDAL TO THE FUCKING METAL

I'm the driver's seat of my life, and I'm not fucking afraid to take the road less traveled. I can take whatever roads I want to take, say, "Screw it," to the map, and floor the gas pedal no matter how many roadblocks I encounter. It's my damn foot on the pedal and my hands on the wheel, and I will not allow any bullshit backseat drivers to try to tell me where to go. I am steering toward my future, so either enjoy the ride or bail the fuck out!

I WILL SHINE BRIGHT AS HELL

Regardless of how I feel, whether I'm strong and resilient like a diamond or fragile like a piece of glass, I am still shining. I am still beautiful, and I will continue to sparkle and shine with fucking brilliance. I am a powerful, determined woman, and I will not let anyone dim the light that shines from my soul like a fucking beacon. I am unstoppable, unquenchable, and I will not be undermined by any of the bullshit this world has to offer. I am a diamond, I am glass, and I will continue to shine.

I WILL DROP THE DAMN INSECURITIES

Fuck the haters and fuck my insecurities; I will not let them stop me from going for what I want. I'm done letting my past failures define me; instead I'm going to prove them wrong and take the chance to show what I can do right now, today. I'm strong, powerful, and capable of standing the fuck up no matter how many times I might get knocked down. I'm taking back my life and inspiring others to do the same. I will not let my insecurities keep me from living my best life and succeeding.

I HAVE A WEALTH OF FUCKING RICHES

I am rich from all my life experiences. I can't help but be proud of the bumps and bruises I've endured, for they have only made me smarter and that much fucking stronger. I stand here today, cashing in on my victories and unflinchingly embracing my imperfections with a fierce sense of pride and overwhelming determination. I am damn grateful for the lessons I've learned and earned, and I won't take a single moment of this beautiful shitstorm life for granted. I'll keep on pushing through every challenge that comes my way.

I WILL FUCKING PERSIST

I'm a badass woman who will never give up on achieving excellence. I'm not chasing perfection, but I'm willing to put in the effort and never-ending perseverance it takes to get there because I know that a journey well traveled is a journey well-lived. Failure doesn't scare me; it only makes me work harder. I'm not afraid to swear my head off when I'm pushing myself, because that's how I know I'm trying my best. I'm determined to see my dreams come true, and I won't let anything stop me from getting there.

I AM UNSTOPPABLE AS FUCK

I'm so strong, powerful, and unwavering that it astonishes even my own damned self from time to time. I know my own limits, but that just means that I'm sure as shit ready to defy them. I'm not scared of or intimidated by difficulty. Instead, I'm ready to take on whatever comes my way, and I'm sure as hell not going to let any fucking thing stand between me and my goals. I'm here to make the impossible possible, and I'm going to show the world what I'm made of. I'm ready to exceed my own expectations and make my fucking mark.

I. FUCKING. MATTER.

I solemnly swear to this truth: I matter so damn much. My dreams, goals, and aspirations are my own and are not for anyone else's consumption. I will not be denied my happiness or my success. No one can stop me from pursuing what I want, and no one can take away my own damned voice. I will never let anyone tell me that I am not worthy of my own dreams, nor will I allow anyone to take away the power that I have to make them a reality, because I am a badass fucking queen, and I will never forget that. This life is mine and I am doing it for me.

I WILL EMBRACE THE DAMN SHITSTORM

We all make mistakes, and we all fail sometimes. But if we deny ourselves the chance to fail, we deny ourselves the opportunity to learn and grow. So don't be afraid to take chances, even if it means failing. Fuck perfection. Fuck the fear of failure. Embrace the mess. Embrace the lessons. Embrace the opportunity to learn something new. We are all capable of greatness, and we all have the ability to succeed beyond our wildest fucking dreams. So don't be afraid to take risks, and don't be afraid to fail. We can still be amazing, even if we don't get it right the first time.

I DESERVE FUCKING RESPECT

Respect is earned and owned, and I will fight fucking hard for it. I will never back down from the challenge of standing up for myself (even to myself), no matter how difficult it may be. It might not come naturally at first, but damn it, I'm up to the task, and I will make sure that I do what is necessary to get the respect that I fucking deserve. I won't let anyone step over me or take advantage of me; I'm here to stay and won't let anyone tell me otherwise. This is my life, my voice, and my body, and I will use it to demand the respect that is due to me—no matter what.

FIERCE AS A MOTHERFUCKING TIGRESS!

My true self is unapologetically fierce. I am a hell-raiser, a force to be reckoned with. I'm going to do it my way, and to hell with anyone who doubts me. I've got fire and bravery in my veins, and I'm not backing down. I'm going to stand up, take this life by the balls, and make it my own. And I'll be damned if I apologize for doing it. From this moment forward, I'm going to be the strongest and most powerful me I can be, and I'm going to swear and kick and scream and fight for it. My true self is not defined by anyone else, and that's a damn good thing.

HIGH OR LOW, I'M A BAD BITCH AT ANY ALTITUDE

I'm done with comparing my life to others—I will let my own highs and lows be the barometer for my success. Whether soaring in the clouds or picking myself up from the dirt, my accomplishments and failures are both mine to own. If others try to pass judgment on me? Fuck them and all the bullshit they throw my way. I'm badass, powerful, and strong, and my life experiences are uniquely mine. No one can ever take away the value of what I have gone through. I'm embracing my journey and the strength that comes with it, and I'm fucking proud of it.

I WILL MAKE MY PRESENCE FUCKING KNOWN

I stand tall and defiant in the face of adversity, refusing to go softly through life. I face my challenges head-on, and I'm not afraid to swear up a fucking storm and fight tooth and nail for glory if needed. I will not accept defeat; I will keep pushing until I have achieved every goal I have set for myself, because my victories are the most rewarding when they take the most effort. I am a powerhouse, and I will not be silenced. I will shout my truth from the rooftops and make sure everyone hears my voice. I am here and I am ready. I will not go gently through life—I will go fiercely.

BEAUTY IS IN THE EYE OF THE BEHOLDER, AND THAT'S FUCKING ME

I am not beholden to anyone for my self-worth. I am mine, and I will swear by it. In the face of any challenge, I will remember that love for myself is infinitely more valuable than love from another person. I will not allow anyone to dictate my worth or worthiness, but instead take ownership of my own. I will learn to care for my own needs and wants, and in doing so, I will be better equipped to share my love with someone else. I will always remember that I am worthy, and I will love myself with a fierceness that others can only admire and never take away.

I WILL LET MY FIRE BURN BRIGHT, BITCHES

I am a woman of fire and ferocity. Even if I feel safest and most comfortable at home, I will still push myself out of my comfort zone and seek new adventures. I will not be cowed by fear or doubt, but instead embrace the unknown with a powerful fierceness and fuck-yeah attitude. I will relish the chance to try new things, to embrace the unfamiliar, to grow and experience life to the fullest. I will take risks, take charge, and take the lead. I will live life with a passion and intensity that few can match. I am a woman unafraid and unyielding. This is my promise to myself.

I'M LEARNING TO SAIL MY FUCKING SHIP

I'm a damn goddess and I won't take no for an answer. No shitstorm, no matter how fierce, can break me. No situation, no matter how difficult, can stop me. I may make adjustments, but I sure as fuck won't back down, nor will I ever give up. I'm capable of weathering any storm, and I will continue to fight for what I want and need in life. I'm a powerful, strong, resilient woman, and I sure as fucking hell got this shit!

I TRUST MY MOTHERFUCKING INSTINCTS

I am a focused bitch who is comfortable in my own skin and unafraid to follow my own path. I will not try to fit myself into some bullshit mold that someone else has created for me, but rather listen to my own instincts and do what brings me joy, pleasure, and happiness. No matter what I do or who I am, I sure as fuck will never be ashamed of who I choose to be or the decisions I make that result in my being happy.

I WILL MOTHERFUCKING MANIFEST

I swear by the outstanding fucking power of my own intentions: I will create my own reality, and I will revel in the joy that comes from it. Today, I will gleam with the happiest of happy, and there's no force in the fucking universe that can stop me from doing so. I am me in every way it is possible to be, and I'm ready to take charge of my own life. Cheerfulness will be my companion and guide today, and I'm ready to take on whatever comes my way.

I WILL RISE AND FUCKING GRIND

I refuse to be held back by any obstacle, be it internal or external. I will not be taken advantage of or silenced. My heart is filled with courage and determination, and I will not let anything stand in my way. I will no longer wish for things to happen; instead I will fucking make them happen. I will take action and drive forward with passion and conviction, striving to achieve greatness and refusing to be held back by any bullshit circumstance that might arise. I will do the fucking work, and I will succeed.

I KNOW THE BEST IS YET TO FUCKING COME

As the seasons change, I will remember that nothing is permanent. The hard times will pass, and my struggles will improve. Change is right around the corner. I fucking swear it. No matter what hardships I face, I won't be broken or discouraged. I will stay patient and determined, and I will find that I can press on. I know that the universe has something better in store for me right around the corner, and I will damn well make it happen. I know that I am worthy of success, and I will fight for it.

WORRIES CAN'T FUCKING HOLD ME BACK

I don't have time for doubt, and I don't have the luxury of worrying about what the world thinks. I know that my life has meaning. I'm going to stand up, flip the world two middle fingers, and keep being the same bad bitch I've always been. I'm going to keep pushing, fighting, and believing that I am enough because I have the power to use my badassery to my advantage. I'm going to fucking own it, and I'll do it with a smile and a laugh in the face of any asshole who tries to tell me different.

I AM WORTHY AS FUCK

You don't have to be perfect to know that you have worth. You don't have to have it all figured out to have something to offer. You can be a fucking mess and still be a fucking force to be reckoned with. Your life has a meaning that is uniquely yours, and you can find it in the everyday moments. You don't have to understand the big picture to recognize your own value. So stand tall, move with purpose, and never forget that you are fucking worth it.

LET'S HEAR IT FOR FUCKING DEFENSE!

My courage is a force field that surrounds me like an impenetrable fucking shield. While I am within it, I refuse to be intimidated by any obstacles that come my way, transforming them into challenges that I can conquer. I use my weaknesses as tools to build greater strength, wrapping myself in layer upon layer of experience like damn armor, and my fear is channeled into action. I am unbreakable, and no one can fuck with me so long as I continue to believe that is true.

I AM FIERCELY FUCKING FREE

I will not be weighed down by the bullshit expectations of those who seek to control me. I will not submit to the bindings of society that aim to keep me down nor be restrained by the words and opinions of those who seek to keep me in my place. Instead, I will take a step away from the things that have been holding me back and look forward to the future with a newfound confidence and strength. I will laugh in the face of those who doubt me and swear to never let anyone limit me. I will strive to break the chains of my past and move forward full of passion and purpose!

I WILL TAKE CARE OF MY DAMN SELF

Listen up, ladies: I know it's hard, but it's high fucking time to take care of ourselves. Loving ourselves is more important than anything else, and it is only when we can fully embrace our needs and desires that we can truly spread our love to others. So don't be afraid of telling people to bugger off while taking a stand for yourself; let that passion be a source of strength. You are ferocious, you are unlimited, and you are enough. It's time to show yourself the same love and respect you give to others. Don't be afraid to swear by it.

I WILL FUCKING GO FOR IT

I stand at the precipice of my life and confidently proclaim, "I own this shit!" I have struggled, and yet I will not be cowed. I have been told to be smaller, to settle for less, to accept half measures and scraps, but I will not. I will be bold and unrepentant, asserting my worth and refusing to take no for an answer. I will not be shamed for being ambitious, for dreaming big and speaking truth to power—especially when that power is bullshit. I refuse to accept any status quo that doesn't suit me. I will fucking make something of this life. I own this!

I CHOOSE FUCKING JOY

Happiness is whatever I feel it is. Fuck the world and what it tells us we need or don't need. My happy place is right here, with me. I will be loudly, joyfully me, singing at the top of my lungs and not giving a damn about what anyone thinks. I will not spend all of my energy trying to make others happy. I will splash in all of the puddles, laugh out loud at the rainbows, and dance like no one is watching. I am my own unique self, and no one can take that away. This is the power of being a woman—to take up space, to claim our damn joy, and to live life on our own terms.

I WILL LET MYSELF BE A FUCKING BEGINNER

My life is only just beginning, and I will not let anyone, including myself, hold me back from the vision I have. I swear on every ounce of my beautiful badass being that I will not be deterred. I own my life, my present, my past, and my future. I accept the challenge of life, and I will not be intimidated by it or any poor soul dumb enough to stand in my fucking way. I will not just accept but relish in being a damn beginner at something. No matter what, I will not be defeated. I am worthy of greatness, and I will create the life that I want.

I WILL EMBRACE THE POWER OF REST, DAMN IT

Today, I choose to honor my own fucking needs and give myself a necessary break. Like fresh ink on paper, I am choosing to take a rest before turning the page. I am in control, and I will not let exhaustion take over. I will be damn gentle with myself and use this time to care for my body and spirit. With fierce love and determination, I will not let anything stand in the way of my well-being. Today is a fresh start, and I will replenish my energy so that I may rise up tomorrow with a clear mind, rekindled fire, and open heart.

FUCK REPUTATION, FUCK GOSSIP; ONLY I DECIDE MY WORTH

My reputation is the least important thing about me, and I say, "Fuck it," if you think it defines my worth. My accomplishments and failures do not define me—I define me. I am so much more than the judgment of others, more than their expectations and opinions and whispers. The course of my badass life will not be determined by outside forces, pushed around, or made to feel small. I will stand tall, give my best fuck-you smile, and carry on in spite of what anyone else has to say about me. I am indomitable, and most importantly, I am me.

I AM A FIERCE FUCKING FORCE OF NATURE

I will not be underestimated. I have an immense capacity for love, passion, and ambition, and I am multidimensional as fuck. With the array of talents and perspectives that I bring to the table—I am a unique individual who has a distinct, beautiful story to tell. I am an outspoken powerhouse, ready and willing to make an impact on this world. No matter what comes my way, I will never give up—I will continue to fight for what I believe in and keep working to make my dreams a reality. I am a storm of potential, ready to rip across this world and change the landscape in my wake.

ONE DAY. TWENTY-FOUR HOURS. ZERO FUCKS GIVEN.

Today I'm embracing being a badass woman, and I'm ready to take on the day. I'm going to seize every opportunity, make the most of these twenty-four hours, and be fucking awesome. I'm going to focus on the positive, put my energy toward what's available, and make shit happen, having the faith and positivity to believe that I have the power to make a difference. Today is the day that I'm going to leave behind any worries, doubts, and fear, and choose to be bold and courageous enough to accept myself. By combining my strengths and my weaknesses, I can be the best damn version of myself possible!

I AM A MOTHERFUCKING GIFT

My love and respect for myself is absolute and un-fucking-flappable. I will never allow anyone to belittle or diminish my self-worth. I am empowered, and I sure as shit know my gifts like I know my own name. No one can take away my pride in who I am, and I will never let anyone's opinion of me undermine my own. My self-love is a fierce and unyielding force, so damn anyone to hell who doubts it.

MY NEEDS HAVE FUCKING VALUE

I fucking deserve love. My love for myself is a treasure that no one can take away. It is infinitely more valuable than love from someone else. When I embrace my own needs and wants, I am better able to give love to someone else. I don't need anyone else to validate me, because I know my own worth. I am enough. I am worthy of self-care and love. I am worthy of setting boundaries and having them met. I am worthy of respect and admiration. I am fucking unstoppable.

FINE AND REFINED AS FUCK!

I swear by the truth of my own soul: I will never stop refining who I am. Every moment of my life, my true bad bitch self emerges more and more. I am a woman of strength and ambition, capable of anything I choose to be. I will never let outside forces define me, for I am the uncontested master of my own identity, and no fool or dumbfuck can take away the power I have to create my own destiny. I will forever be free to choose who I am and who I will be.

I BELIEVE I CAN SO I FUCKING WILL

I will never stop believing in myself. I will never doubt my ability to accomplish my goals and strive for greatness. My thoughts and feelings are valid, and I will never let anyone make me feel less than the extraordinarily capable boss bitch that I am. I will be my own biggest cheerleader and remind myself of the strength and resilience that has gotten me this far. This is the power of believing in myself, and it's something that no motherfucker can take away from me.

I'M A DAMN WINNER

I don't need any ribbon, any trophy, or any certificate to tell me that. I know that the dedication and effort I put in are leading me to greater things. If I don't see the results right away, that's okay—I have faith that my hard work is taking me somewhere better. Nobody is going to take away my confidence and pride in myself, so fuck it—let's keep pushing and move forward with our heads held high. We're winners, and you can bet your ass that we're going to keep winning.

MY KICK-ASS POWER IS WITHIN

My soul is a fucking fire—blazing with strength and beauty. I am inherently deserving of rest, joy, and love. I will never settle for anything less than what I am worth, instead demanding from the world and those in my life that they treat me with the respect and love that I so clearly fucking deserve. The universe supports me, and I refuse to be held back from achieving my wildest hopes and ambitions. My soul is a stunning damn work of art, and I will never forget the power and worth that comes from within.

I WILL LIVE WITHOUT FUCKING REGRETS

Today I'm done apologizing for who I am. I'm done trying to make sense of my emotions. I'm done seeking permission or justification for my decisions. Today, I'm fucking taking charge. I'm doing what feels right in my heart, without a second thought, guilt, or unnecessary explanation. No one can tell me what to do or how to live my life, and that's okay. I will do whatever the hell I want, with no regrets and no apologies. This is my day, and it'll be fucking awesome.

BLESS THIS FUCKING MESS!

It's time to kick ass and take names! I'm living my life on my own terms and reveling in my own successes and struggles. No one else can define my worth or define what is important to me. I'm taking control of my own destiny and embracing this messy, beautiful, badass journey that I'm on. I'm not here to compare myself to others but to show up as the best version of myself and find strength in my own process. I'm a bad, bad bitch, and no one will ever shake my faith in that fact.

HELL YEAH, I CAN OWN MY HABITS

This week, I'm going to break the bad habit I've been meaning to break. I'm going to make my future self proud. I'm going to show myself and all the other incredible people I know out there that we are alive and have the power to grow and evolve. Every day I will take small steps in my routine that will have a lasting lifelong impact. We're not here to stay stagnant or be held back by anyone or anything—this is our time to refine our behavior, cultivate who we want to be, and make our own paths. Let's show the world who the fuck we are!

PERFECT IS THE ENEMY OF AMAZING—AND I DON'T NEED MORE FUCKING ENEMIES

I am completely, totally, 100 percent fucking done beating myself up for not living up to some imaginary standard of perfection. Perfection is the worst kind of bullshit. For not a single second longer will I allow myself or anyone else to set impossible expectations for myself that I'll never be able to meet. It's time to focus on the beautiful fucking miracle that is my life and to start embracing what is right in front of me, right now. I'm strong and capable, and I can make my life whatever I want it to be. So here's to letting go of the impossible and creating something beautiful.

I RECOGNIZE MY DAMN TRUTH

I stand in my power and refuse to be made invisible. It's more than okay to ask for external affirmation if I so choose, but I know that I am strong enough to affirm myself too. I know that my worth is not defined by anyone else's bullshit opinion of me. I'm done allowing others to define who I am. I'm done with trying to fit into someone else's idea of success or beauty. No matter what anyone else says, my voice matters most and my truth is unquestionably fucking valid. So yes, it's all right for me to seek out external validation sometimes, but I won't allow myself to be diminished by anyone else's opinions.

I CAN AND WILL FUCKING SURPRISE MYSELF

I refuse to settle for anything less than I deserve, and I will not be bound by the expectations of others. I am competent, adaptable, and capable of so much more than anyone else can even begin to fucking imagine—even me. I will push myself to learn and grow, and no barrier or bullshit limitation can stop me from succeeding. My strength is unbreakable and my ambition is unstoppable. I won't let anyone or anything stand in the way of my growth, not even myself. I will give myself the room to take risks, make mistakes, and keep striving until I reach my damn goals.

DUMBFUCKERY CAN PASS ME BY

I know that sometimes it feels like the all the fuckery of the world is rallied against me. But I will not be disheartened. I will take the high road and not take things personally, like the fucking queen I am. The way people treat me is often a reflection of their own issues, and I can choose to not let it bring me down. I will strive to stay focused, no matter how hard it gets, because fuck that noise! Instead, I'm going to keep my head up, stay positive, and not let anything stop me from achieving my goals. This is my fucking fight, and I'm going to win.

I WILL LISTEN TO MY FUCKING BODY

I will not be dissuaded from taking care of my health and listening to my needs. My body is my temple, and I will defend it as fiercely as any warrior priestess. I may bend but I will never fucking break when it comes to respecting my body and its cues. My body is one of my most precious assets, and I will always be thankful for it. I will pay close attention to what it tells me, nurture it with healthy habits, and protect it with fierce love. No one else has the right to dictate how I care for myself.

I AM IN-FUCKING-VINCIBLE

I will never apologize for who I am or what I stand for. I will not be told to be small, to take up less space, to be meeker. I'm an amalgamation of my experiences, my scars, my beauty, and my strength. And. That. Is. Fucking. Powerful. The next time I am looking for peace, I will create a moment of silence and strength. I will take care of myself today and every day—because that is the only way to make sure the world knows what I'm made of. My serenity exists in moments of silence and in moments of power.

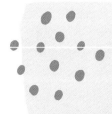

I AM MY OWN GREATEST FUCKING CHAMPION!

I will not let anyone else fight my battles for me. I am a motherfucking warrior queen, I'm in charge of my own destiny, and I'm going to fucking seize the opportunities that come my way. No one can do that for me, and no one can take away my power to make it happen. I'm an unstoppable force, and I won't let anyone stand in the way of my success. My determination is fierce, my rage is something to fear, and I won't rest until I get what I want. No more waiting around for someone else to make it happen—it's time for me to be a badass and take control.

THE BEST BASTARD TO BE IS ME

I'm done with trying to be what other people want me to be, and I'm done pretending that I'm someone I'm not. I'll be me; you be you. It's human nature to want acceptance and validation from others, but I know in my fucking heart that the only acceptance and validation that truly matters is what I give myself. So tonight, I swear to myself that no matter how hard it gets or how much external pressure there is, I will remain true to the brilliant bitch I am and stand by my own integrity and happiness. No one else can give me the satisfaction of knowing that my life is being lived on my own terms—only I can do that.

I WILL GET STARTED BY FUCKING STARTING

Just beginning some shit seems like the hardest part, but that won't stop me. I refuse to be fucking deterred by the time or detours it takes to bring my ideas to life. Even when seen as impossible, I will push through and never give up in the pursuit of making my dreams come true. I will persevere through every bullshit setback and fucked-up circumstance the world throws at me. I'm unstoppable, unbreakable, and will make shit happen no matter what it takes. Instead of focusing on how far away I am from my goal, I will take the first step and begin.

I WILL LOVE MYSELF FIRST

I will never apologize for the bad bitch aura and ambition that defines me. I will never be ashamed of my power and my potential, even if the bullshit noise of the world around me sometimes tries to mute it. I'm not here to apologize for who I am or what I can become—I'm here to swear by it. My relationship with myself is the foundation of every other fucking thing in my life. If I want to succeed, improve, and move forward with my goals, then I sure as hell need to prioritize that relationship first. My journey starts and ends within me, and that's the best damn project I'll ever work on.

MY POTENTIAL IS DAMN NEAR ENDLESS

I'm fucking sick of the world telling me I'm not great. I'm done being afraid to be who I am and own my greatness. I won't let anyone stand in my way of achieving my potential, because it is fucking boundless. Because of that, I won't allow myself to be afraid of working hard and fighting tooth and fucking nail for what I want. If I put in the effort and persevere, nothing can stop me from being great. So fuck fear and fuck doubt, because with dedication and courage, I know that everything I fucking need for success is already in me, bitches!

I BELIEVE IN MY DAMN VISION

I can have anything I want if I just choose to believe it is possible—so it is! No matter the obstacles or bullshit societal expectations, I can break through them and achieve whatever I want. It's just a matter of giving up the fucked-up belief that I can't have it or don't deserve to have it. This isn't a pipe dream; this is my life, and I'm going to fucking own it. That's why I choose to believe in something bigger than myself and never back down from my goals. So if you're standing in my way, step aside or get run the fuck over, because nothing is stopping me now.

I WILL SEE THE FUCKING MAGIC

I know that life can throw some real curveballs and fuckery at us, but I'm not going to let worry stop me from seeing the wonderful, magical shit that also exists. I'm going to keep being inspired by what's around me and recognizing all the good there is in life, because damn it, there's a fuck-load of it! I won't let worrying distract me from the beautiful little things, divert me from my dreams and hopes, or keep me from being truly present. In every moment, there's an opportunity for magic.

I AM A CONFIDENT BITCH

I am so damned done with letting a lack of self-esteem hold me back. I'm done being paralyzed by uncertainty. I'm done doubting myself and playing it safe. From now on, whenever I feel the urge to act, I'm going to fucking go for it! No matter what the outcome may be, at least I can say that I tried my damnedest and didn't let fear stop me from giving it my all. From here on out, no more holding back—it's time to take action and be fierce!

I WILL RECONNECT AND FUCKING CHILL

I'm allowing myself to take a break this weekend and give myself some damn well-deserved rest! I'm not going to feel guilty about taking a timeout from the hustle and bustle. It's my damn right to stay in my pajamas all day if I want, and I'm going to do it with a smile and a full heart knowing that I am worthy of rest. This weekend is about me, my well-being, and reconnecting with the things that make me feel good. So let's just kick back, relax, and enjoy the hell out of this stay-in-pajamas-all-day type of weekend!

I'M TRYING MY DAMN BEST

Today, I'm embracing my badassery and recognizing my worth. I'm giving myself permission to be vulnerable and courageous, to take risks and make mistakes. I'm allowing myself to feel my emotions and not be ashamed of them. I'm doing the hard work to become the best version of myself, and that's something I can be fucking proud of. No matter what the world tells me, today I choose to practice self-kindness. I'm trying hard and doing my best, and that's enough—because it's all I can ask of myself.

"FOLLOW THE LEADER" MEANS "I FUCKING GOT THIS"

No matter what anyone else may say, I am strong, brilliant, and effective. This power crown will never come off my gorgeous damn head. I'm going to keep pushing boundaries and breaking through obstacles, no matter how hard it gets. My strength is undeniable, and my ambition is unshakable, and fuck you to anyone who questions either of those facts. I'm here to take charge and make things happen—to be a leader who isn't afraid of making mistakes or going against the fucking grain. There's nothing that can stop me from achieving my goals and living my best life because when I'm on top of my game no one is more powerful than me.

RING THE BELL, BITCH;
I'M WINNING THIS PRIZE

Today, I'm going for the damn prize. I have the knowledge and the know-how to make it happen, and I'm not afraid to get my hands a little dirty if need be. I'm going to break through any barriers in my way with a stubbornness that'll make my enemies fucking cower in terror. I know what I'm capable of, and today, I'm using that power to propel myself forward. No matter how hard it gets, no matter how tough it gets, no matter how much it feels like the world is against me, I will never forget my strength or back down from a challenge. Today, shit's getting real.

MY SELF-CARE ISN'T FUCKING SELFISH

Today, I'm allowing myself much-needed breaks, because sometimes I need to rest before taking the next step. My body and mind will sure as hell thank me later. I'm not giving in to the bullshit pressure, but rather giving myself permission to take a break and regenerate. I can damn well do that. I'm taking my time and respecting the journey of self-care, because this is my damn life and it's important to honor it. I'm not letting anyone else dictate my pace; only I get to decide when to rest, when to work hard, and when to push through. Today, I choose rest and regeneration—and that's fucking awesome!

I WILL GO WITH THE FUCKING FLOW

I don't need to predict the future to fucking own it. I know that the world can be full of bullshit and unpredictable chaos, and it's easy to get discouraged when things don't go exactly to plan. Life happens when you're busy planning, and I will remember that I still have control over my choices, even if things don't fall into place perfectly. I'm not going to dim my light, let fear of the unpredictable affect me, or change course because of a few shitty hiccups. I will ride that damn wave!

SAYING NO IS A FUCKING SUPERPOWER

I am not a damn failure because I say no or step away from anything that is hurtful to me. I am a success for taking care of myself first. I'm going to do me! It's about damn time that I start prioritizing my own well-being and making sure I'm safe and sound. No more playing second fiddle to those who are harmful to my own growth and peace of mind. It's time for me to take initiative and break free from the binds of any negative energy or toxic relationships. It's time for me to say no when I've had enough or done too much, and realize that my self-care comes first, no matter what!

I PICK MY FUCKING BATTLES!

I am not afraid to admit that I don't have all the fucking answers, and that's okay. I don't have to win every battle to know I'm worth something, damn it. It takes courage and strength to recognize when it's time to move on and focus on a new challenge. I'm not afraid to swear by it—I am perfectly fucking fine not mastering all challenges. Not every conflict can be won, but that doesn't make me any less badass. I will recognize when it's time to move on and face a new battle with courage and resilience.

FREE SPEECH 101: FUCK ALL THE HATERS

I refuse to ask fucking permission to be myself, and I'm done with letting anyone or anything else try to make me smaller. I unequivocally, wholeheartedly reject the dumbass idea that I have to censor my thoughts, feelings, and actions in order to be accepted. That is not what it means to be a woman. My worthiness doesn't depend on other people's opinions of me. It's time to break free from the shackles of society's expectations and start living my life with intention and purpose. Fuck anyone who tries to tell me otherwise—I'm going to make my own rules, speak my truth, and stand firmly in who I am. This is my journey and no one else's.

I CAN STEP OUTSIDE THE FUCKING BOX

I refuse to let my past failures define me or hold me back from trying new things. I am capable of so much more than my insecurities tell me, and I'll be damned if I don't give myself a chance to prove that. I won't let my doubts stop me from taking risks and exploring the unknown. I am strong, I am powerful, and I will not be held back by my fears. I will step out of my comfort zone and into the exciting world of possibilities that are out there waiting for me. I am ready to take charge of my life and show the world what I'm made of!

INSTINCTS OF A FUCKIN' WOLF!

I will trust my own intuition, no matter what any dumbfuck may think or say. For too long I've second-guessed myself and worried about the judgment of others. Not one fucking day more of that bullshit. I'm done giving myself away to outside opinions that don't serve me or my fucking goals. Instead, I'm going to have the courage to listen to my gut, take risks, and make decisions for myself. That's the only way to get closer to what makes me truly fucking happy.

KINDNESS IS MINE AND IT'S BADASS!

I am worthy of love and contentment, and I will no longer accept anything less than what I deserve, because I'm fucking awesome! No matter how hard life may be, I will always embrace the kindness that comes my way—it's a reminder that there are people out there who understand and appreciate me for all that I am. My worth is not determined by anyone else's opinion or actions; it belongs to me alone. So, on those days when self-doubt creeps in, just remember: you're fucking amazing, and you deserve happiness and joy. Don't ever forget it!

I HAVE GRIT AND FUCKING GRACE

I trust in my ability to conquer whatever life throws at me. No obstacle is too daunting for me to overcome. I will not be disheartened if progress isn't immediate and I might have to work hard for it. I have the courage and the grit to tackle anything, no matter how long it takes me. I'm not scared of hard work or of failure; instead, I use them as fuel to keep going and keep pushing forward. With every step, I am becoming stronger, more resilient, and more confident in my abilities. My success is inevitable, so bring it the fuck on!

I AM OPEN AS HELL TO WHAT'S NEXT

I accept that I don't need to control the outcome of change. I will stay open and receptive to whatever comes my way, no matter how hard it may seem. I trust that even if things don't turn out the way I expect them to, I will be able to take something away from the experience and use it to push me forward into new levels of badassery. I am too fucking ferocious to allow my fear of the unknown or of failure to keep me from embracing change and all that comes with it—good and bad. I'm ready for whatever life throws at me with courage, resilience, and a shitload of perseverance!

I AM SURROUNDED BY AMAZING BADASSES

I am thankful as all hell for my loved ones, because they provide me with a foundation of acceptance and support that allows me to fucking shine. Even when I feel down, they are there to pick me up, remind me of my worth, and fill me with the strength to keep going. They provide an anchor that helps steer me away from destructive thought patterns and toward a life that is full of love, joy, and possibility. Their encouragement gives me the courage to take risks, try new things, and reach for a brighter future. Without them I'd be lost in the choppy waters of life—but with them I am damn unstoppable.

I DON'T NEED TO HAVE ALL THE FUCKING ANSWERS

I'm done trying to make sense of it all. I don't have to know life's meaning in order for my own existence and experiences to be meaningful, damn it! Instead of searching endlessly for the answer, I will focus on what matters most—myself. So fuck anything that tries to keep me from believing that my presence has value; this truth is mine alone, and no one else decides its worth. I can make the most out of the shit in front of me. Today marks a new beginning: one with strength, confidence, courage, and self-love guiding each step forward into an empowered motherfucking tomorrow!

I AM BRINGING THE FUCKIN' THUNDER!

I am an un-fucking-stoppable force of nature, as beautiful and terrible as any thundercloud or blizzard. I will not be held back by anyone or anything, sweeping over the land until I get whatever the fuck I desire. No petty bullshit like doubt, fear, or fatigue can stop me from achieving my goals. I know that when I set my mind to something and stay focused, nothing can stand in my way. My power is limitless and my ambition is unending. I will never give up on myself or succumb to the lies of the world that tell me what I cannot do.

I CHOOSE FUCKING KINDNESS

Today, I'm going to remind myself to be fucking kind—to others and myself. To cut myself some slack, because I'm trying and doing my best, damn it, and that's all that matters in the end. I'm not perfect and that's okay; it's okay to be human. So even when things don't go according to plan and I start to feel overwhelmed, I won't beat myself up or stress out over it. Instead, I'll take a deep breath and speak words of encouragement to myself. Fuck society's standards; fuck anyone who tries to bring me down; fuck anyone who doesn't believe in me or my dreams; fuck anything that doesn't serve me in the long run.

I PUT MY FUCKING HEALTH FIRST

No matter what horseshit the world throws at me, I'm not going to let it break me. I'm going to swear and shout and fight my way through it, because I know that focusing on my health is the only way to stay strong. Whether it's nourishing my body or my mind, I will do something today that's good for my health. I will take time to take care of myself, giving myself permission to be kind and gentle with myself. I will make self-care a priority and forgive myself for any mistakes I make along the way. I am a fucking warrior, and no one can take away my power to choose wellness for myself.

I WILL USE MY FUCKING VOICE

I will not be fucking silenced. I will never be cowed into quiet submission, made to shrink or retreat. My words are my own, and they damn well deserve to be heard. I won't let anyone try to bully me into being quiet, and I won't take any shit from anyone who tries. Today and every other day, I will stand up for myself and speak my truth, no matter how uncomfortable it may make others. I will never stop fighting for what's right, and I won't be shamed for having an opinion. No one can take away my power or my right to speak out. That's a fucking promise—and a threat.

I AM THE FUCKING GOAL

I will not be denied. I will not be disrespected. I will not be fucking diminished. The most rewarding goal I will ever work on is me, and I won't let anyone stand in the way of that. My relationships, my career, and my personal goals do not define me—they are only a reflection of who I truly am in my heart. To move forward, I must first foster self-love and self-respect, recognizing that I am worthy of success and capable of achieving it. To improve my relationships, my career, and move forward with my personal goals, I need to focus on improving my relationship with myself first—for only by doing this can I truly become the most badass version of myself.

NO COMPROMISE, NO BULLSHIT

No matter what, I'm not going to give up my self-respect and contentment for someone else's approval. I'm going to be me, and that's all I need to be. If other people don't like it, that's their fucking problem, not mine, because I'm done living life on someone else's terms. I won't settle for anything less than what I deserve, and that means standing up for myself when it counts. So fuck it—if someone can't accept me as I am, then they don't deserve me at all. My happiness is too valuable to compromise on, and no one else can give me the validation I seek—that has to come from within.

STARTING IS HARD, BUT NEVER BEGINNING IS FUCKING WORSE

I will never forget that starting something is the hardest part. I won't let my dreams remain stagnant or let those naysayers get me down. Instead, I'm going to take that first step and not give a fuck about how far away I am from my goal. I'm going to let my ideas come alive and turn into reality, no matter how hard it may be. I'm not just going to talk about it; I'm going to do it! Fuck fear, fuck doubt, and fuck the status quo—because if there's one thing I know for sure, it's that greatness is born from taking risks.

SLOW AND STEADY, KICK-ASS GROWTH IS THE WAY

I'm on a journey to understand myself, and I couldn't be prouder of the progress I'm making. Even when things don't seem to be going my way, I'll never forget that progress isn't always linear. I'm fucking fierce and brave enough to keep pushing forward, even when the path is winding and unpredictable. I'm capable of so much and deserve to give myself some damn credit for all the hard work and effort I put in. When things get tough, I'll remind myself that my journey is a marathon, not a sprint. Here's to me embracing all the progress, no matter how small or big it may seem!

STAND BACK, I'VE FUCKING ARRIVED

My power is relentless and un-fucking-deniable. I have the strength to overcome any obstacle and achieve anything I set my sights on. I alone am in control of my destiny, and no one can stop me from getting what I want once I decide I want it. My ambition is unshakable and my drive is unmatched—fuck anyone who thinks otherwise. I am powerful beyond measure, and if I want something, it's only a matter of time before I make it mine. Nothing can stand in my way, and no one can hold me back. So bring it on world—I'm ready to make you my bitch!

I AM JOYFUL AS A MOTHERFUCKER!

I am responsible for my own joy, and I will not be ashamed in seeking it the fuck out! I will no longer be content with settling for anything less than what I truly deserve. It's time to take control of my own happiness and not let anyone or anything get in the way. I swear that from this day forth, I will do whatever it takes to find and maintain my joy. Whether it's taking a break from obligations or cutting out toxic people, I won't rest until I find what brings me true satisfaction. My joy is mine and no one else's, and they can't take it away from me. Here's to embracing the beauty of self-love and to never again settling for anything less than pure blissed out joy!

LIFE IS 10 PERCENT THE SHIT THAT HAPPENS AND 90 PERCENT HOW I REACT TO IT

I'm done apologizing for who I am and how I choose to live my life. My road to success is paved with setbacks and failures, but you can bet your sweet ass that won't fucking stop me. I won't define myself by my mistakes; instead I'll use them as inspiration. I can't control what happens to me, but damn it, I can control how I respond. So I'm going to keep pushing forward and building the life that I deserve—the life where I don't just accept my failures, but learn from them. That's how you become successful—not by avoiding mistakes and setbacks, but by embracing them and using them as a source of damn strength!

BURN, BITCH, BURN!

Today, I'm feeling that brilliant goddamn bonfire inside me, roaring high and telling me that it's time the world heard the sound of my voice. I'm going to tap into my true feelings and take a closer look at my authentic self, confident that that self is a badass who deserves the world. I know what I want, and more importantly, I know what I don't need in life. I'm going to intentionally curate a life that's full of love and joy, and fuck anyone who tells me otherwise. It's time to embrace my true power and show the world what an amazing woman can do when she puts her mind to it!

I AM WORTHY AS A MOTHERFUCKER

I am not perfect, but I know that I am sure as shit worthy of the love and admiration of those around me. Whether it be my family, my friends, or even a stranger, I will stand firm in the knowledge that my worth is something that is inherent in me. No one can take away from the fact that I am strong, stunning, and deserving of some goddamn respect and love. And while sometimes it may be hard to believe in myself, I will never let doubt stop me from embracing the love that so many have for me. In moments of struggle and pain, I will remind myself with pride: I am worthy of their love!

I AM ON TOP OF MY SHIT

I am empowered, confident, and self-assured about the things I know. There's no bullshit here; I own my shit. My voice is mine and my worth is mine to determine. I'm bold and unapologetic in my power, with a fuck-it-all attitude that won't be silenced. Even in moments of doubt, I'm growing and learning what it means to be self-assured in the face of adversity. My strength knows no limits—I'm unstoppable and ready to take on any challenge that comes my way. No matter the outside influences around me: I determine who I am and what I'm worth—not anyone else.

BRING IT ON, ASSHOLES!

This is my truth: I am a woman of strength, fortitude, and determination. I wholeheartedly accept every experience that comes my way, even the difficult ones. I will not shy away from challenges, but instead embrace them with an open heart and say, "Thank you very fucking much; may I have another?" I understand that sometimes the lessons they may provide might not be easy to learn, and I give myself permission to feel whatever wonderful, fucked-up emotion comes with it. Even when it hurts and frustrates me, I will remain strong and remember that these hard times are what make me stronger. This is my fucking truth!

MY ASSHOLE ANXIETY DOES NOT CONTROL ME

I will not shrink back in fear in the face of bullshit anxiety. I will stand tall, challenge my anxious thoughts, and ask myself if my fears are rational or a result of panic. I will not let my worries consume me; instead, I will confront them with a fierceness that only a badass queen like me can possess. I am unafraid to challenge the status quo and question what fuckery society tells me to be afraid of. So screw fear, screw anxiety, and screw anyone who tries to tell me otherwise; I'm ready to take on the world with my head held high.

EVEN BAD BITCHES NEED BREATHERS

Today I will give myself permission to take a break, to show myself compassion, and to allow myself to be a goddamn human for once. I will not be ashamed of my imperfections or apologize for them. Instead of striving for perfection, I will focus on doing the best I can with what I have. You can bet fucking money that I recognize that greatness isn't something that is achieved overnight; it's something that comes with dedication, resilience, and often a bit of luck. Instead of wasting my energy worrying about what tomorrow may bring, my goal is to make sure that when tomorrow arrives, I am ready to both receive it and embrace it.

I AM A GODDAMN HAMMER IN A WORLD FULL OF NAILS

I trust myself, and I sure as hell have all the tools and abilities that I need to make my own decisions, even if they are unconventional or unpopular. No one can tell me what's right for me—only I know that, and only I can decide it. That makes me powerful as fuck! My ability to think critically about how a decision will affect my life is an invaluable strength of mine. No matter how hard someone tries to steer me in another direction, ultimately this power belongs solely to me. With practice comes confidence, and with every day my self-trust grows stronger within me, as does faith in my intuition—because when push comes to fucking shove, nobody knows better than me what's best for me.

SHINE, QUEEN, SHINE!

I will be unapologetically myself, always, and never dim my beautiful, boss bitch light to fit in or to please anyone else. I won't compare myself to anyone else, and I will never let anyone else's opinion of me define my self-worth. I refuse to let fear stop me from being unique, memorable, and proud of who I am. Fuck them all if they can't handle my energy; they don't deserve a part of my story anyway, and my personality is too damn precious to be overshadowed by comparison and criticism. So here's to bucking the status quo, living life on my own terms, and loving the hell out of myself just as I am!

I MOVE LIKE A MOTHERFUCKING BOSS!

I am the master of my own destiny, and I will not let anyone else dictate how I treat myself. I will stand strong in my convictions and keep the promises that I made to myself, no matter how small. Whether it's drinking a glass of water as soon as I wake up or taking a short walk today, I'm going to hold myself accountable with every ounce of my being. My word is sacred, so fuck you if you think I'll break it! Nothing can stop me from achieving greatness because if there's something worth doing right now, then damn it, girl—let's get out there and do it!

CAN'T KEEP ME THE FUCK DOWN

No matter what fuckery this life throws at me, no matter how dark or difficult the situation may seem, I will never give up. I refuse to dwell in self-defeating thoughts and feelings of despair. Instead, I choose to boldly remind myself that there's always light waiting for me at the end of this tunnel of bullshit. When times get tough, when it feels like everything is crumbling around me, I swear by my own strength; these are the things that will help me reach the sun rising on a better day. It's time to take back control of this journey—let's go!

MY ATTITUDE IS FUCKING GRATITUDE

Today I am taking care of myself. I am embracing the power that I have to be kind to myself and others, no matter how hard the day may be. With my head held high, I will not let any obstacles stand in my way. I'm going to take a deep breath and swear to myself that no matter what, I'm going to take control of this day, on my own damn terms. I will start today off on the right foot with a fucking attitude of gratitude for all that I have and all that is coming up ahead. No matter what comes up today, I commit to being kinder to myself and others.

I WILL BE THE DAMNED CHANGE

Today I am going to own my damn power and make a difference in my corner of the world. I don't have to conquer the whole world in order to make an impact—even the smallest actions can have a huge effect—and I'm done with waiting for someone else to take charge. Today, I'm taking matters into my own hands and becoming a badass force for change. No challenge is too big for me, and no obstacle will hold me back from making the world better for myself and those around me. It's time for all of us to take ownership of our lives and be brave in our pursuit of progress and justice. Let's fucking do this!

FRESH START? FRESH AS FUCK

Life is a story I write in pencil, and I'm damn empowered by that fact. Nothing I do is ever set in stone—no matter how much shit life throws at me—so if something doesn't go my way, that's okay. I always have the chance to erase and begin again with fresh eyes and a fiercer determination than before. No one can take away my power to start over as many times as necessary until I fucking get it right. That's what makes me strong enough to face whatever comes next without fear or hesitation: knowing that failure isn't final—it's just part of the process.

PERFECTION CAN PISS OFF

I am perfectly imperfect, and I'm done apologizing for it. My quirks make me unique; my flaws make me strong. I will never be ashamed of who I am, because that's what makes me a badass woman. I have the courage to own up to my mistakes and learn from them without letting them define me. No one can take away my power or tell me how to live my life—only I know what's right for me, and that is something no one can ever deny. So here's to embracing all the weirdness and swearing like a fuckin' sailor—because this is exactly who I choose to be!

I AM FUCKING GOLDEN

I am glorious and radiant—to hell with what anyone else says. I have so much inside of me that only I can appreciate, more than any outside gaze or opinion could ever hope to understand. My worth is not defined by the world around me; it is defined by my own power and potential that lies deep within this badass body. No matter how hard others may try to make me feel small or insignificant, I know in my heart that I am capable of greatness beyond their expectations. The fire that burns inside of me will never be extinguished no matter how many times someone tries to douse it with doubt and fearmongering.

SHATTER THESE DAMN SHACKLES AND CHARGE INTO TOMORROW!

The time is fucking nigh to take charge of my life and start living the life I want. No more waiting for the perfect moment, no more putting it off until tomorrow. I am a damn powerhouse, an unstoppable force, and I will not be held back by self-doubt, fear, or any other bullshit concept. It's time to break free from the chains of self-doubt and fear that have kept me from living my life on my own terms. Today I embrace the power of choice and take ownership of my life. It's time to move out of my comfort zone, live authentically, and unapologetically chase after what makes my heart sing. Fuck fear—it's time to start living!

PASSION AND PRIDE ARE FUCKING PRIORITIES

It is not only brave and badass; it is essential to prioritize your own happiness and joy. You deserve a life that makes you feel alive and fulfilled. Don't wait for joy to come to you—go out and find it yourself! You have the power to own your own life and make it what you want it to be. So go out there and fucking chase after the joy that will make you feel like the amazing woman you are. Embrace your passions, take risks, don't be afraid of failures—they only lead to more successes. And above all else, remember: focusing on your own happiness is not a selfish act; it's necessary.

I WILL GET THE HELL OUT OF MY OWN DAMN WAY

I will not be fucking beaten, either by myself or outside forces. No matter how strong the opponents standing in my way, I won't give up on myself or anyone else. I know that the world isn't always looking out for me—but that doesn't mean I'm going to fucking sit back and take it lying down or stop trying. It can sometimes feel like every jackass in the world is united against me (even me), but no matter what comes at me, I will never stop fighting for who I am and what I believe in. There are times when it feels impossible to keep going, but every day I will push through, no longer holding myself back.

NO REGRETS, MOTHERFUCKERS

I won't waste a second of my precious fucking time on regrets. I'm always making the best decisions I can in each moment, and that's all anyone can do. So fuck it—let's make those decisions with power and intention! No more second-guessing ourselves or allowing others to control our paths. We know what we're capable of, so let's take charge of our lives and own every single choice we make. Let's be unapologetic about who we are and never forget how much strength lies within us as women. Because when we show up for ourselves fully, there is no limit to what we can achieve!

MOVE, BITCH, GET OUT THE WAY!

I'm a woman who sure as shit won't be deterred or defeated. I will fight for what I want and what I believe in. No one can take away my dreams, my ambition, and definitely not my fucking desire for success. I am empowered to do anything and everything that I set out to do, and all those in my way had better move or get run the fuck down. My faith in myself is unshakable; no matter the challenge, I have the strength, the resilience, and the courage to overcome them all. This is who I am and this is what I believe in: that anything is possible if you put your mind to it and never give up on yourself.

I'M MY OWN DAMNED BEST FRIEND

I am comfortable with knowing that the most important relationship I have is my relationship with myself, and I damn well better be. This means recognizing that I can't depend on anyone else to make me feel worthy or whole; it's up to me, and only me, to build self-worth and confidence. That doesn't mean shutting out all support from others—far fucking from it! It just means having faith in myself enough to know that whatever happens, no matter who comes into my life or leaves it, I will always be okay, because at the end of the day, loving myself comes first. So let's get this straight: you're goddamn amazing! Now show yourself some love!

EFFORT OVER OUTCOME, AND FUCK THE HATERS!

Today, I'm reminding myself to just do my best and embrace the results, whatever the fuck they may be. I'm done with beating myself up because it's not good enough. Whether things go wrong or right, I'm going to give it my all and own the fuck out of it. I won't let shame or self-doubt hold me back from putting in my best effort. I'm taking the plunge and trusting that whatever comes out of it will be something worth celebrating. No matter how hard it gets, I'm not going to give up on myself or my dreams. I'm going to keep pushing through and make sure that every day is chock-full of badassery!

ON MY FUCKIN' HAZMAT SHIT!

I am a badass woman who refuses to let anything stand in the way of my own self-care and well-being. I won't be shamed or cowed into remaining in situations that are harmful to me. I'm done with that toxic shit. Instead, I'm taking action and succeeding at putting my own self-love and respect first. No more settling for less than I deserve. No more tolerating toxicity, particularly toxicity disguised as love. It's time for me to start living my best life, and that starts with me taking care of myself first, no matter what anyone else says or thinks. Fuck it all—I'm stepping away from anything that isn't good for me and embracing the success of knowing that I've chosen myself first.

SEE THE FUTURE, BE THE FUCKIN' FUTURE!

I stand tall and proud, knowing that I have the strength and courage to make my vision a reality. This might take time, but I am ready to take on the challenge with determination and tenacity. I will not let the naysayers or dumbass haters bring me down, because my optimism is ever present, and I will not be deterred from my mission, no matter what life throws at me. I am over-fucking-flowing with hope and excitement for all that's ahead of me, because I know that each step I take is bringing me closer to the vision I have for myself. In this moment, nothing can stop me from fulfilling my potential; nothing can stop me from becoming who the fuck I want to be.

I HAVE BIG FUCKING PLANS

I am the leader of my life, and I have dreams to fucking fulfill. I'm flipping that script and writing my own damn story! No one knows what's best for me like I do, so it's time to take control and make sure this narrative is about *me*. It's up to me to choose how I want things in my world to be. Who gets a seat at the table? What are we striving for? Where will our paths lead us next? So today—no more waiting around or playing small—let's get out there, speak truthfully with passion and conviction, and create whatever change needs creating. Time to put these big fucking goals and plans into motherfucking action!

I WILL LEAN INTO THE DAMN SUNSHINE

Just like flowers turn to face the sun, so too do I find strength when looking for the good before dwelling on any badness in this world. Life can get tough at times, but that won't stop me from being true to myself despite any bullshit or nonsense going on around me. And anyone who tries to steal my sunlight? They can go fuck themselves. No matter where you come from or whatever situation you're currently facing—know your worth and own it unapologetically; let nothing hold you back from shining brightly each day as a beautiful flower blooming under the sun's rays!

EVEN BAD BITCHES NEED A MOMENT

I am powerful in my body, fierce and unwavering. I'm not afraid to say, "Fuck you," to haters or to stand up for what's right. In moments like these, when I'm feeling a little overwhelmed by everything going on around me, I take five minutes to just be with myself. To remind myself of my strength and fortitude. To feel the wind against my skin and let it soothe me as I take a deep breath and exhale every ounce of bullshit and doubt and fear that threatens to weigh me down. Now more than ever, women need each other; we must look out for one another, show up for each other no matter what comes our way.

PAUSE, MOTHERFUCKER; I'M DOING ME

I will enjoy small moments of silence today. If those moments have been hard to find lately, I will tell the world to wait a fucking minute and intentionally create one for myself. This will be one small moment to remind myself that I'm fucking capable, strong, and brave enough to take on whatever life throws my way. No matter how difficult things may seem right now, I'll keep moving forward with grace and confidence in the knowledge that I can handle anything.

DON'T FEAR THE FUCKING YEAR!

I will no longer allow the difficulties of this year to bind me. I'm done with feeling like a victim, and I refuse to be held the fuck back by what has already been. This is my time for reinvention and renewal—to take control of my life and realize that I am powerful beyond measure. It's time to step into my truth as a fierce woman who knows her worth, speaks her mind, and doesn't give a fuck about anyone or anything that tries to stand in her way. Here's to leaving the past behind me, embracing the present moment, and forging ahead on an incredible journey full of growth and transformation.

LIKE A BADASS JULIA CHILD

Today I will whip up a batch of generosity, positivity, kindness, and self-love. That is the recipe that will bring me the most joy today. So let's get cooking! Today I choose to be fiercely generous with my time and energy, to spread love and show up for myself and others in powerful fucking ways. Let's fill our minds with positive thoughts about ourselves—no more self-sabotage or doubt allowed! And let us never forget how badass we are when it comes to loving ourselves unapologetically. Don't just take my word for it—practice some radical self-care today, throw on your favorite outfit, break out into an impromptu dance party if you feel like it—whatever makes you feel most alive!

I AM A WARRIOR PRIESTESS, AND THIS BODY IS MY DAMNED TEMPLE!

I will not be fucking ashamed of loving and nurturing my body. My physical health is a priority, always has been, and always will be. I don't give one single fuck about what anyone else thinks—this is for me! Every day, I commit to making decisions that honor the needs of my mind and soul, as well as those of my physical self: eating healthy foods that make me feel good inside and out, getting enough restful sleep every night so that I can wake up feeling energized each morning, exercising in ways that bring joy rather than exhaustion into life—all with love guiding the way toward a healthier, more badass me!

I AM A GODDAMNED MIRACLE

I am alive, and that is nothing short of fucking remarkable. I don't need to do anything else today in order for it to be a success; living my life authentically and being present in the moment are more than enough. I trust myself completely—even when times are tough or things feel impossible—knowing that whatever lies ahead will only make me braver, wiser, and more badass as a woman. Today's journey may not take me anywhere extraordinary, but it has brought me right here: safe at home with all the power within me to live fully without apology or shame.

HARD TIMES PASS, BUT MY STRENGTH IS FUCKING ETERNAL

I am unflinching, unwavering, and resilient as all hell. I know that this difficult time will pass, like all things do eventually. Right now, it's hard to remember that everything is only temporary, but I swear to myself: no matter what fuckery comes my way today or tomorrow—the good times and the bad—I won't give up on myself. My strength comes from within me and only grows with each challenge faced head-on, and I know that nothing can keep me down for too long! This moment of bullshit is just a short phase in life that will soon be behind us, so let's get ready for whatever lies ahead!

FORCEFUL AND NOT FUCKING REMORSEFUL

Today, I will be a force to be reckoned with. Whenever I feel stressed or down, I will stand up and shake it off like the badass bitch that I am! No matter what comes my way, no obstacle will stop me from rising above and moving forward. Movement is my superpower today—a power that can never be taken away from me. When the going gets tough, I'll get going and dance it the fuck out like nobody's watching! Nothing can derail me when I take control of my body and mind, and use them as tools for self-expression instead of letting stress bog me down. Today is mine to seize; let's fucking go!

I DON'T NEED YOUR FUCKING APPROVAL

I'm not asking for anyone's goddamn permission to live my life on my own terms. I don't need approval from anyone, and I won't let other people dictate when or how I should do things. My success is entirely up to me, and I fucking own it. No one else can determine what makes me happy; that's all down to me too. Whatever timeline works for me is the right one—and fuck anyone who tries to tell me differently! It's only by following my heart that I can reach true fulfillment in life, so here's to blazing a trail of joy and progress at whatever pace suits me best.

DON'T CROSS THESE FUCKING LINES

My boundaries are goddamn sacred and I will honor them without a moment's fucking hesitation. When I say no, it is an emphatic declaration of self-love that I refuse to compromise. My no is a powerful fuck-you to anyone who tries to take away my agency over my own life; my refusal is an act of reclamation, a sign of autonomy and strength. Saying no doesn't make me mean or selfish; on the contrary it shows how much respect and care I have for myself, which far surpasses any other sentiment out there.

OXYGEN MASK IS FIRMLY IN FUCKING PLACE

I will not apologize for loving myself first. I am a woman of enormous fucking worth, and I deserve my own praise and respect. I'm not asking for anyone else's permission or approval—I'm cutting through the bullshit and fully embracing my power, both internally and externally. I swear by this—I am a fucking badass and no one is going to tell me otherwise. Try to deny me my own love and respect at your own peril—it might just be the last fucking thing you do.

KICKING ASS AND TAKING INITIATIVE!

Today I will own my power and take initiative, no matter what. Whether that means speaking up in a group, taking ownership of a task or leading a new project—I can fucking do this! I am strong enough to face any challenge head-on and courageous enough to go for it. It may be hard, but I'm ready to step up and make shit happen. My strength comes from within, and nothing is too big for me to handle—because if there's one thing that's true about me, it's that I always rise above and come out on top!

TIME IS ON MY FUCKING SIDE

I will be patient with myself and trust that even if things aren't working out right now, it doesn't mean they never will. Time is a powerful force—it can bring us great joy and blessings, and I'm damn sure not going to give up on myself before giving time the chance to do its thing! I am worthy of growth, success, and everything else life has in store for me. So no matter what happens today or tomorrow, I know that eventually things will work out for the better, because better is what boss bitches like me deserve.

I GET KNOCKED DOWN BUT GET RIGHT THE FUCK BACK UP!

I am a woman, and I won't be kept down by any fucking person. I will stay strong and focused on making it through today. Greatness is within my reach, but I must be careful to not overwork myself to the point where I can't see it or appreciate it. When tomorrow comes, I'll start fresh and new with a fiery determination to not just survive life's bullshit, but thrive. Even when life knocks me down, I will find the strength to get back up and keep pushing forward. And for anyone who doesn't believe in me? Fuck you; you don't matter anyway.

RIGHT NOW, TODAY, THIS FUCKING MINUTE

I'm ready to take my life into my own hands, and today is the fucking day I start! No more letting days pass me by. Now's the time for me to stand up with confidence, strength, and fierceness like never before. I get to decide what kind of energy goes into this day—no one else has that power but me. From now on, if it doesn't align with what I want in life, then fuck it—I have no time for anything that harshes my fucking flow. Today marks a new beginning where I have agency over how each moment will shape itself, and whatever direction they lead toward is mine alone to choose!

PRODUCTIVITY CAN WAIT A DAMNED MINUTE

I am worthy of time for self-care, and I won't let my need for productivity take that away from me. Today, I'm going to give myself a goddamn break even if I don't think it's necessary. This isn't just about taking some time off; this is about recognizing the value of caring for myself and investing in my well-being so I can continue to do amazing shit with my life. My mental health matters, and today, no matter what anyone else says or thinks, it's going to be a priority.

I AM A FUCKING SPACE-MAKER

As a woman, I give myself permission to live powerfully and authentically. I know that the more I create space for others to do the same, the easier it will be for me to step into my own power. I'm fucking done with holding back and denying who I am—it's time to show up as my true self and live unapologetically. My voice matters, and by using it I give others permission to do the same. Now is my time to shine bright, speak boldly, and make shit happen.

LITTLE VOICE?
MORE LIKE LITTLE ASSHOLE

I am a badass, powerful woman, and I will not be held back by my self-doubt and fear; instead I'll use it as motivation to reach new heights and push the boundaries of what I'm capable of. Every time that little voice in my head tells me, "You can't do this," or "You're not good enough," I will remember that it's just a sign that something great is on the horizon, and take one step closer to achieving my goals.

TWENTY-FOUR HOURS
OF ME OWNING THIS SHIT

This morning I get to choose what I will feel, do, and be when I walk out the front door. Just watch me fucking show up today like a badass woman ready to take on whatever comes my way. No more waiting for permission or validation from anyone else—today is about owning who I am and claiming my power with grace and ferocity. This is *my* day, and no one can fuck it up, because I refuse to give them the right. So here's me stepping into my greatness with all that I fucking got!

MISS ME WITH THOSE BULLSHIT MISGIVINGS

I am a powerful woman, and today I will wholeheartedly choose to let go of the bullshit limiting beliefs that tell me I'm not creative, smart, or strong enough to share my whole self with the world. Instead, I'm embracing my boldness and determination today—nothing can stop me from doing what I set out to do! My badassery is unrivaled, and it's time for me to show the world exactly how brilliant and brave I truly fucking am.

NUANCED AS A MOTHERFUCKER

Today, I will let go of outdated, bullshit black-and-white thinking. I recognize that there is no one single path to success or understanding; rather, there are a multitude of perspectives that deserve to be respected and appreciated. As a woman, I sure as fuck have the courage to stand up for what is right even when it's difficult. With this power, I refuse to accept any bullshit that stands in my way today—no matter how daunting or intimidating it may appear. Instead of striving for perfection, I strive for inclusion—recognizing that everyone has something valuable to offer.

I AM UNFURLING MY DAMN WINGS

I stand strong in the face of fear and doubt, always believing that I have the power to shape my own future. To me, it is as if I am holding a baby bird—delicate but full of potential—cupped between my hands. For now things may seem precarious, dangerous, but given enough time and love, I know that this bird can grow into a badass fucking eagle! Today is the day that I take to the fucking air and fly!

YOUR PROBLEMS ARE NOT MY FUCKING PRIORITY

I will not be discouraged by the doubts and shitty insecurities of others. Instead, I will look inside myself to find strength, power, and joy. I will seek happiness within my own heart, allowing myself to take up space in this world with confidence and courage. As a woman, I refuse to let anyone silence me or make me feel small for speaking out against inequality or injustice. My voice is powerful and valid—fuck anyone who tells me differently! Now is the time for self-love, and it's my fucking turn to shine brighter than ever before!

YOUR EGO IS NOT MY FUCKING PROBLEM

I will not allow anyone to make me feel inferior for the sake of their comfort. I am capable, creative, and powerful in ways that don't always fit into bullshit traditional definitions of femininity. My inventiveness and sense of humor are part of what makes me badass, and they're easiest to access when I practice self-love because they remind me that I have a lot to offer this world—no matter who else may disagree or be intimidated by it. So fuck 'em! Nobody can take away my worth or limit my potential, because I'm worthy as fuck just as I am right now.

I WILL NOT BELIEVE THE DAMN IMPOSTOR SYNDROME

Today I choose to live with intention and joy. Life is short and nothing is guaranteed, so it's sure as hell up to me how much of this gift I'm going to use. So, no more excuses; now is my time! Fuck the fear that keeps telling me, "You can't do this," or "It won't work." Screw impostor syndrome, comparison traps, and self-doubt—from today on they don't get a say in what I am capable of doing. Today marks the day when I decide for myself who gets access to my life—it's time for action. Let's go kick some ass!

I AM CALM IN THE DAMN CHAOS

My mind is like a mountain lake, calm and cool and majestic as fuck—and with it I am able to handle anything that comes my way with ease. No matter what storm clouds move over these peaks, you can bet your ass that nothing can shake me from this powerful stillness within myself. So long as I am calm in my heart, I can move through the most fucked-up turmoil with grace, confident that in time I will find the answer to even the craziest of life's problems.

ONE BREATH, ONE STEP, ONE BADASS BITCH

I will not apologize for taking up space. For just five minutes, I will walk outside and let the wind kiss my skin and the sun warm my face. I will take a deep breath and be unapologetically me. My body is mine to own—it's part of who I am, an integral piece of my identity that cannot be taken away from me or diminished by anyone else. So fuck what they say; with every step forward, every breath in and out, I'm reclaiming ownership of myself.

CHECK THIS SHIT
WHILE I CHECK MY LIST

I choose to be fueled by my to-do list and not overwhelmed. I know that every task on this list is a way for me to take ownership of my life and create something fucking amazing. No matter how big or small the tasks are, they remind me that I am the one in control—no one else can dictate what power or success looks like for me. Each day, through these accomplishments, I build self-confidence and strength within myself as an empowered woman swearing fuck yes at every challenge ahead!

TAKING SPACE AND IN YOUR DAMN FACE

I will take up space every single day—no more shrinking myself down, making myself small and invisible to give assholes room. I have goals, dreams, and desires that must be fucking honored if I am to live a fulfilled life. To hell with any and all who would deny me my rightful place in the world; from now on, there's only one way forward. It's time for me to claim what is mine by birthright—power, strength, and self-determination—so here's me declaring loud and proud: this body of mine isn't just taking up space but claiming its spot among equals!

I'M THANKFUL EVERY FUCKING DAY

Today, I will be bold and show the world my authentic self. Fuck labels and expectations, because I defy all labels. In a world where so much is out of my control, today I'm grounding myself in gratitude for all that exists within me—from the changing of seasons to the breath in my lungs to simply being alive. My body is strong and capable; it's carried me through moments both happy and hard with grace. No matter what life throws at me, or how many times people try to put boundaries on who they think I should be—fuck them! The universe has blessed me with this beautiful existence as an incredible person worthy of love and respect.

NO DAMNED APOLOGIES, ONLY GRATITUDE

I will not apologize for the woman I am. My flaws, struggles, and imperfections are part of my identity; they make me unique and outrageously powerful in ways that no one else can be. No matter what shit anyone says or thinks about me, I refuse to shrink away from these parts of myself—they have made me who I am today! Nothing can take away from my power as a strong individual with an unwavering sense of self-love, so fuck it all if someone doesn't like it. The truth is, this world needs more brave women like us to break down barriers and lead change—so stand tall on your own two feet, beautiful warrior, because we got you!

GLUE, MEET GODDAMNED RUBBER

As a woman, I am reminded that while I cannot control the words and actions of even the dumbest of fucks around me, I have the power to choose how they affect me. My strength is found in my fortitude: no matter what comes my way, I can dig deep within myself and find an inner calm that will not be broken by any obstacle or individual. With every interaction, big or small, good or bad, friendly or hostile—it's up to me to decide if this experience strengthens my spirit of self-love and acceptance. Fuck anyone who tries to stand in opposition!

ONLY I KNOW MY FUCKING JOURNEY

Today I will embrace my power. No more will I let other people's judgments and expectations dictate who I am or what is expected of me as a woman. Fuck the haters; they're not living in my shoes, so their opinions don't matter anyway. With this newfound freedom comes an understanding that, while it's important to look out for myself and stand up for what matters most to me, it is also essential to give others the same space—free from judgment—to be their true selves without fear or intimidation. It feels damn good when someone has your back like you have theirs—today let us all create that kind of trust amongst ourselves!

I AM ASSET MOTHERFUCKING #1

I am un-fucking-questionably my own most valuable asset. Today and every day from here forward, I will proudly and fiercely protect and nurture my health, just as a mother would care for her child. Even when it feels like all the bullshit of the world has aligned against me, I will never let anyone or anything stand in the way of taking care of myself, because I fucking deserve it! My health is sacred and deserves to be treated as such. I refuse to be complacent in unhealthy situations. So here's to me, appreciating and protecting my health like a goddamn boss!

AMBITION? MORE LIKE I-AM-BITCHIN'.

I am a bold and ambitious woman—and I fucking love that about myself. Not for a single second will I shrink back in fear or be silenced because of outdated bullshit expectations of what my gender should do or be. No matter what fuckery society serves up, my voice is valuable and important; it deserves to be heard. My strength comes from the people who surround me—they love powerfully and give completely without expecting anything in return. They make space for me to grow, learn, and thrive; in turn, I strive to do the same for them too. Together we are an unstoppable fucking force that cannot be ignored!

I AM THE SILVER FUCKING LINING

I will boldly create my own peace and actively experience life today. I refuse to allow fear or self-doubt keep me from living the fullness of each and every second! In moments when fuckery looms and darkness clouds over, I am strong enough to acknowledge what is real but brave enough to reframe it with a positive outlook. Through all the chaos and uncertainty that comes with being alive, I choose resilience as an act of love for myself—a reminder that no matter how fucked up things are right now, they won't stay this way forever.

TO HELL WITH PERFECTION, I'M HERE TO GROW

I will not be perfect, nor will I ever strive for it—but I will sure as fucking hell chase excellence, effort, and perseverance with all my heart and soul. I will not be deterred by obstacles or hardships; I will remain steadfast and committed to my goals. My ambition and determination will be unmatched as I rise to any challenge, refusing to give up until I have achieved the excellence I seek. I am a woman who will never quit, I will never surrender, and I will never settle for anything less than that which I have worked so immensely fucking hard for.

THIS GRIN IS MY FUCKING GAME FACE

I will do something today to make myself smile. I'm going to let that warmth fill up my chest and then spread it around like wildfire, damn it! My strength as a woman is unshakable; no matter how hard the world tries to bring me down, I know who and what I am—a badass beauty with an abundance of love in her heart. And every single day, from this moment on, I'm going to use that power for good: be brave enough to speak out against injustice and lead by example so others may follow suit. Today isn't just about making myself feel good—it's about reminding the universe why women like me are fucking phenomenal people worth fighting for.

ZERO SHAME, MAXIMUM FUCKIN' FAME

I refuse to be ashamed of my body, my mind, or my emotions. I have the right to speak up for myself and others around me, even if that means telling shitty people to go fuck themselves. When I choose to just be in this moment, without judgment of myself or anyone else, it opens me up to a world of inspiration—one that allows me to give back and shine with confidence and strength. My truth is mine alone—fuck any expectations that don't serve me! And when I'm true to who I am on the inside and out, there's nothing stopping me from inspiring greatness in those around me too.

I'M CONFIDENT, COMPETENT, AND FUCKING READY

I am confident in my ability to take on whatever comes my way today. I'm not afraid of the challenges that await me and know anything is possible with a little grit, grace, and fucking confidence! I will never back down from what stands before me, no matter how intimidating it might seem at first glance. My power lies within, so there's nothing stopping me from achieving greatness or making an impact if I truly put my mind to it. There are no limits holding me back—only those created by myself, which can be broken through self-belief and determination. So here goes nothing: let's do this shit!

COMPLEX WITHOUT A FUCKING COMPLEX

I am a complex and powerful human being who is undeniably worthy of love. I will not apologize for my flaws, struggles, or imperfections; they are part of what make me who I am. No matter how challenging life gets, I can take comfort in knowing that these perceived shortcomings give me an inner radiance able to overcome any problem put before me—this is the beauty of being uniquely myself! My vulnerability is my fucking superpower; it allows me to create meaningful relationships with those around me while connecting deeply with myself too. From now on, I'm embracing every fucking inch of my complexity!

I CAN DO THE DAMN THING

I will own my badassery and embrace every challenge that comes my way. I'm a fucking dynamo who is capable of anything, and nothing can stop me from achieving whatever it is I set out to do! When obstacles arise, instead of feeling stuck or discouraged, I'll remind myself: "This isn't an obstacle—this just requires some creative problem-solving!" Whether it's personal growth or professional success, no goal is too big for me to conquer. Every moment presents an opportunity for greatness; all that's required on my part are grit, creativity, and determination. So here goes nothing!

I AM FUCKING BEAUTIFUL ON THE INSIDE TOO

I am a kind human being who is fucking worthy of love. Despite the lies I may have been told in my life, despite all these voices that said I wasn't enough—I am more than capable and deserving of being loved. My worthiness is not a question; it's beyond doubt or debate. Many people around me recognize this truth about me and express their admiration for who I am and what I bring to them—they know how much beauty there is inside me, waiting to be unleashed into the world!

LIBERATED AS A MOTHERFUCKER

I am the ultimate fucking decision-maker in my life. I choose how and when to use my time, energy, and resources—no one else gets a say unless I damned well give it to them. My self-worth is not dependent on anyone else's approval or demands; what matters most is that I'm holding myself accountable for living an empowered life of integrity, intentionality, and authenticity. It's fucking liberating knowing that by owning this responsibility, nothing can ever hold me back from creating the impactful future over which only I have control!

HOPPING OFF THIS FUCKING STRUGGLE BUS

Today I choose to prioritize love and understanding in the face of struggle. No matter how hard it is, no matter what people say, I will not let my struggles define me. Instead, I'll take a stand for myself—and others like me who are fighting similar battles— by embracing acceptance and compassion first. Despite everything that's trying to hold us down or tear us apart, we can still be strong together by leaning into our empathy with grace and grit. We may stumble sometimes, but if we trust ourselves enough to lead with love today, then peace won't elude us much longer. Fuck yes!

SHARP AS STEEL, SWIFT AS FUCKING LIGHTNING

I am a woman of pure, un-fuck-with-able power, and I am not afraid to wield that power as a sword. Even when life throws its most tumultuous storms my way, I remain calm and centered in the knowledge that a peace rooted in power is within me at all times. In these moments, I reclaim control over myself and refuse to allow external forces to dictate how I feel, instead turning inward with confidence to recognize the strength that resides inside every part of me. This inner stronghold allows me to stay rooted even through chaos, knowing that if shit hits the fan, then so be it, because nothing can break this fierce fucking fire burning within me!

I WILL FLY ABOVE ALL THE BULLSHIT

In moments where I don't feel confident, my inner reservoir of strength will always be within reach. This strength is an undeniable truth—it is a fundamental part of who I am that no one can take away from me or diminish. Even if the world tells me otherwise, even if it tries to break down my self-worth with its bullshit standards, nothing will come of it except a resounding "Fuck you"! Because when push comes to shove, nothing matters more than what I believe about myself. That inner belief gives me wings, so whether anyone else believes in my capabilities or not doesn't matter, because ultimately I have faith in all the badassery inside of *me*!

I AM FUCKING CONFIDENT

My self-confidence is a suit of fucking armor that I wear proudly into any battle. No one can take it away from me, no matter how hard the jackasses may try. When life throws challenges my way, I stand strong and unafraid, because knowing my self-worth gives me the courage to face whatever comes with grace and strength. My confidence helps lead me in every decision I make—big or small—because when you are secure in your own power, nothing else in this fucking world can make a dent!

HAND ME MY FUCKIN' BINOCULARS

I am determined, unafraid, and sure as shit ready to take on whatever life throws at me. I refuse to be intimidated by the unknown; instead, I choose to harbor a love of curiosity and adventure. My strength comes from my willingness to explore—it is a flame that burns brightly in the darkest of life's jungles no matter what problems arise or how much fuckery may come my way. With courage and genuine love of adventure as my foundation, I remain open to discovering new things about myself and the world around me with an unwavering sense of wonderment.

GRACE, CHARM, AND BAD BITCH STYLE

I am a woman of astonishing grace and adaptability, and I will not be fucking disrespected or diminished by anyone for any reason. I know that my experiences have made me who I fucking am today—capable, courageous, and ready to make every day my bitch. No matter what has happened in the past, no matter how difficult it may seem right now—I can heal from these struggles because I have learned that every experience is an opportunity to grow into something even more powerful than before.

I AM WALKING MY OWN FUCKING PATH

With every decision made, with every step taken by this beautiful fucking body, I'm taking control over my life because this is *my* path to walk and nobody fucking else's. So today I choose courage over comfort and progress over perfection. Each day forward requires putting one foot in front of the fucking other, no matter how daunting a task may seem at first glance—but I'll be damned if there isn't beauty found when we push ourselves beyond our limits anyway!

I AM THE DAMN DEFINITION OF A *PARTY PERSON*

I will celebrate every fucking win, no matter how big or small, whether it's giving myself a damn pat on the back for having an amazing conversation with my coworker or going out of my way to get some exercise. And when it comes to learning from life's lessons? Fuck yeah! That shit deserves recognition too, because no matter what challenge is thrown at me, I'm going to find a way through it and a way to grow from it—and that in itself is sure as hell something worth celebrating.

A BOLD HEART FEARS NO NEW START

I will not fucking shy away from starting over. For not a single second longer will I allow myself to be held back by fear of the unknown, or some bullshit worry about being judged for taking a step in a new direction—even if it means going backward initially. As women, we are powerful and flexible beyond measure; our strength is unrivaled and can't be overestimated! So let's throw caution to the wind, give zero fucks about what others think, and embrace every opportunity that comes our way!

I Can Change for the Damn Better

I will empower myself to make the changes I want in my life, regardless of what any other jackass may think or want. I swear to myself that I will never accept anyone else's opinion or desire as more important than my own. I will trust my own power to take action and make changes, and stand proud in my damn decisions. I will not be afraid, and I will never doubt my right to make changes in my life—because the power comes from me, not from anyone else.

Call Me Motherfuckin' Monet!

I am the artist of my own fucking canvas. I have been given this life to create something beautiful, meaningful, and powerful with it—not to tear myself down or compare myself to anyone else. My worth is inherent within me; no one can take that away from me unless I give them permission. It's up to me alone how high these walls are built, what colors they are painted, and who gets invited inside—and none of those decisions should be made out of bullshit fear or insecurity but rather through boldness and strength!

CHILL AS A COOL FUCKING BREEZE

I am an awe-inspiring, regal powerhouse. I will embrace the quiet of a winter night, letting go of anything that's been weighing me down—all this bullshit I carry around with me day in and day out. Taking deep breaths, I'll fill my lungs with peace instead: no more guilt or shame for who or what I am; no more fear or worry about things beyond my control. With each exhalation, all these goddamn negative feelings will be released from my body so that strength and courage can take their place within me. My self-love is strong enough to face whatever life throws at me without feeling defeated by it; every breath brings an affirmation of faith in myself as a woman unafraid to show her true badass nature!

EVERY DAY, I ACCEPT MORE OF HOW FUCKING AWESOME I AM

I am on a beautiful fucking journey of self-acceptance. I will not apologize for who I am, and I won't let anyone else make me feel like shit about it either! No more holding back my thoughts or censoring myself because someone doesn't approve. My power lies within myself and my ability to choose how I want to live each day with authenticity and passion. Life may throw curveballs at times, but so long as I stay rooted in self-love and understanding, then nothing anyone says or does can ever stop me from being the happiest version of myself on my own damn terms!

KNOCK KNOCK, MOTHERFUCKER. SUCCESS IS HERE.

I choose to live my life in alignment with my own beautiful courageous fucking morals. I will no longer tolerate settling for a default existence or allowing myself to be held back by outdated ideas of who and what I can be. Life is too damned short, and it's time for me to fucking own my power and take charge! When I let go of the need to force things that aren't meant for me, when I surrender into flow instead, amazing opportunities will come knocking on my door. This isn't wishful thinking—this is an intentional decision based on self-love and trust, one that empowers me every day as a fierce woman determined not only to survive but fucking thrive!

I SHOW UP TODAY SO I CAN SHOW THE FUCK OUT TOMORROW

Today I am giving myself some goddamn permission to take care of me. This world can sure as shit be overwhelming, and that's okay! Every couple of hours today, I will check in with my body and mind, listening deeply to what they need. That could mean taking a break from the hustle or saying, "Fuck no," when something doesn't feel right—no matter what, it's all self-care. By showing up for myself like this, I'm honoring my needs so that tomorrow I can show up even stronger.

MY TRUTH HAS FUCKING FANGS

I am not afraid to speak my truth, and I know that that truth is damned powerful. When someone treats me poorly or carelessly, I do not hesitate to tell them just how and why they should go fuck themselves. They are unworthy of my presence and energy. Instead of wasting time on people who don't deserve it, I choose to confidently embrace the strength within myself to walk away from any situation that does not serve me best. There will always be jackasses who attempt to belittle or invalidate me—but they cannot succeed if their words fall upon deaf ears. My worth lies in knowing when enough is enough.

I RUN THIS SHIT? WE RUN THIS SHIT.

My friends are fellow badasses who help me create a world where we can show up exactly how we are: unapologetically ourselves, stronger together than apart, and determined as fuck to fight for justice wherever needed! These people inspire me daily when they open their hearts fully— loving powerfully enough so that everyone around them feels supported in whatever journey they're on, giving completely of themselves so there's room left over for us all, making space always ready if anyone needs it. These are my beautiful, boss-ass heroes, and they give me courage like nothing else ever could!

LIVE, LAUGH, AND LIGHT THIS BITCH UP!

I will make it a point to fucking laugh three times today. I will watch a funny video, play with my pet, or exchange stories with friends—and no one can stop me! It's up to me to create joy in my life on purpose, because you can be damned sure that nobody else is going to do that for me. The power of laughter reminds us how strong we are, how we can survive even the shittiest of moments when our worlds feel like they're crumbling down around us and still come out smiling. Today is an opportunity for growth and transformation, so let those ugly, uproarious, belly-shaking laughs rip!

KEEP YOUR SAFETY — I'M HERE TO SOLVE GODDAMN PROBLEMS

I don't shy away from difficult situations—I fucking crave them. My strength itself calls them forth so that I may take charge and get shit done. No matter what complications arise, no matter how I have failed before, I can draw on the courage inside of me at any given moment to overcome it all. It's impossible for outside circumstances to define or limit who I fucking am. Within me lies an abundance of bravery, a roaring fire that will never be extinguished as long as there is breath in my lungs. Instead of avoiding hardship, I say, "Bring it the hell on," because nothing will keep me down!

WATCH THE CAPE, BITCHES

Today I am harnessing the power of my heroes, both real and imagined. With their courage as a guide, I will look fear in the eye and spit in its fucking face, swearing never to back down, no matter what adversaries may stand in my way. Today and every day I refuse to be held captive by these false narratives of who or what I should fucking be. Instead, with passion burning bright within me like an unquenchable fire, I draw strength from those that have come before me. With my head held high and my cape in place, I will conquer impossible odds just as they did. And so too shall it be for myself now: unstoppable force meets immovable object—all hail my badass self, Queen of the Fucking Universe!

NO DRAIN ON MY FUCKIN' PARADE

Today, I choose to prioritize my own goddamned energy and time, because it's about time I set some fucking boundaries around what drains me in order to make room for the things that energize me. As a woman, it is not only okay but fucking necessary for me to be discerning about how much of myself—emotionally and physically—I give away each day. This isn't selfishness; this is self-care! So today, with fierce love and determination, no more sacrificing who I am or what sets my soul on fire just so some jackass can benefit from my work or life force!

THE FEAR LETS ME KNOW I'M FUCKIN' LIVING

I know that fear and adventure go hand in hand when I'm following my dreams. You can bet your ass that it can be scary, but that's not a bad thing! When faced with difficult situations or challenges ahead of me, the only way to succeed is by embracing those fears head-fucking-on. So here's what I swear to myself: I will never let anyone stop me from going after what I want in life—no matter how scared shitless it makes me feel. By facing these fears courageously and unapologetically, nothing can stand between my ambition and success!

I WILL LET GO OF THE SHAME AND SHIT WEIGHING ME DOWN

I love the genuine, sincere me. I take no shame in what I am, and I will not allow anyone to define me by what I am not. I will be unabashedly and defiantly me, shining with authenticity to cut through all the bullshit around me. I'm not afraid to tell naysayers to get fucked when I need to, and I'm damn good at that and everything else I do. I am my own person, and I will define myself by all that I am, not by what I'm not.

REAL TALK, REAL SHIT, REAL FUCKING POWER

It's time to reclaim our power and stop fucking doubting ourselves. We can do anything we set our minds to, because no matter what anyone else says, there is nothing that stands in the way of us achieving greatness except our own misgivings! I'm not here for excuses or self-doubt; when it comes down to brass tacks, I'll be damned if I don't get shit done. When I set my mind on something? Shit gets real. I can and will accomplish everything that matters most to me, because this story doesn't end until success has been achieved.

MY VICTORIES BELONG ONLY TO ME!

I am a ferocious, joyous free spirit, and I will not let bullshit like self-doubt or shame encroach on my moment of celebration. No matter what anyone says or does, no force in this fucking world can take away from me the things that I have earned through hard work and dedication. My successes are mine to own—they do not come at someone else's expense, but rather as a result of believing in myself fully and never giving up even when it seemed impossible! Today is just another reminder that I sure as fucking hell deserve everything good coming my way.

ONE PROBLEM. ONE DECISION. ONE FUCKING SOLUTION.

Today, I will make one major decision, and it will be the right fucking choice for me. As I consider my options carefully, allowing both my intellect and intuition to guide me in equal measure, I'll also let go of any bullshit doubts or inhibitions that try to hold me back. In this moment, with all its possibilities laid out before me like a buffet fit for an empress—I won't give myself permission to second-guess what might come next. Instead I swear by one simple, irrefutable fact: today is fucking mine!

I WILL RISE TO THE DAMN CHALLENGE

I am a boss bitch who eats problems and shits solutions. I will not let anyone bring me down. Instead, I will draw strength from the positivity of those around me. I will surround myself with motivated and passionate people who will lift me up and inspire me. Their energy and enthusiasm will become my own, and I will use it to fuel my drive. I will never forget that I am incredible, ambitious, and motherfucking capable, and I will use this energy to take charge of my own destiny.

MY VALUE? INFINITE.
MY STYLE? BAD AS A MOTHERFUCKER.

I am a worthy and infinitely valuable woman who deserves to ask for what I fucking need. No matter how scared or uncomfortable it may be, I choose courage over comfort in situations where my voice should be heard loud and oh-so-fucking clearly. Fuck the fear of rejection—if there's something in life that would make me feel fulfilled, then goddamnit I'm going to go after it with all my might! If someone says no—fuck 'em; they don't get to decide whether or not I should have access to joy in this world.

I AM FUCKING FEARLESS

I am excited to embrace whatever today brings, knowing that wonderful gifts don't always come packaged the way we anticipate. I'm ready to explore and see what this day has in store for me—no matter how unexpected it may be! As a badass woman, I've got faith in myself and my abilities, and nothing will stop me from uncovering all of life's surprises with enthusiasm and tenacity. It's time to go out there fearlessly without any hesitation or doubt— let's fucking do this!

I WILL LEAVE THE PAST IN THE FUCKING PAST!

It's never too late for a good old-fashioned fresh start. I may not be able to go back and undo the past, but that sure as shit doesn't mean that today isn't a new day full of possibilities, and nothing can stop me from creating my own fucking ending! No matter what has come before us, it doesn't define who we will become in our future. We have everything within ourselves needed for success: creativity, passion, intelligence. So let's take this moment as an opportunity to rise above any obstacle or limitation holding us back, because it's time for all of us ladies out there to fucking slay whatever comes next!

I WILL FIND STILLNESS IN THE BUSY BULLSHIT

Even if my schedule feels 100 percent packed today, I can always make space for some damn calm and serenity. No matter how busy life gets, I have the power to create moments of peace in between all the hustle and bustle. It's not a sign of weakness; it's a badass act of self-care that makes me fucking boundless. Taking time out for myself gives me strength and clarity so I can do more with less stress and be even better at what I do. So fuck yes—no matter how crazy things get, there is always room to bring some stillness into my day.

THERE'S FUCKING JET FUEL IN MY BLOOD

I am alive, I am powerful, and this is something to be incredibly thankful for. Every morning I wake up with a new day before me and a new opportunity to show the world all the badass shit I can do! We may have encountered hardships in our lives, but that doesn't mean we give up on ourselves or each other—no fucking way. Instead let's use those experiences as fuel so that together we rise higher than ever imagined possible, because together we are a motherfucking force of nature!

ONE THING AT A TIME, BUT THAT ONE THING IS FUCKING AMAZING!

You can bet your ass that I am powerful enough to do anything and everything, but not all at fucking once! Rather than feeling overwhelmed or defeated by the things that need to be done in a day, week, month—whatever it may be— I will prioritize my time accordingly so that I don't feel like shit trying to take on too much. There is no shame in pushing some tasks back until tomorrow; this world needs me more energized and focused rather than exhausted from taking on too much today.

I RUN AT MY OWN DAMNED PACE

I will take complete ownership of my actions and hold myself accountable for them, but fuck you if you expect me to run myself ragged in the process. Promptness is a virtue that I value highly; however, so too is patience with oneself—something many people are not taught to have. This doesn't mean embracing shit like procrastination or stagnation! It just means giving ourselves permission to make mistakes and learn from our experiences without feeling like we have failed entirely if things don't go as planned. So fuck it, let's give ourselves some grace today, because we sure as hell deserve it!

EFFORT OVER EXPECTATIONS, EVERY DAY OF THE FUCKIN' WEEK

I won't beat myself up if I don't meet a certain expectation. That's fucking bullshit, and it isn't fair to me or what I'm capable of doing! Every day is different—some days will be better than others—but no matter what, the most important thing is that I'm always trying my damn hardest in everything that comes my way. My best looks differently on each given day, and all I can do is strive for my personal excellence regardless of how much shit life throws at me.

MY FLAWS ARE FUCKING BEAUTIFUL

I'm learning to embrace and love myself, flaws and all. I refuse to hide behind a mask of perfection, because there is an awesome power in my imperfections. The truth that lies beneath my surface may be hard for me to face sometimes, but it's also what makes me bold, brave, and strong as fuck! My beauty comes from within; no one can take away or diminish its worth. It's time I recognize this strength inside of me—each part has an inherent value, regardless if others like them or not! These parts have been neglected for too long, so today—and every day—I choose some damned self-love over shame!

TODAY, TOMORROW, AND YESTERDAY — I SLAY THIS SHIT

I am proud of my determination and resilience in the face of adversity. Every damn day I rise, show up for myself, and work hard to become a better version of me. That alone is something to be fiercely fucking proud of. No matter what life throws at me or how many bumps there are along the way, nothing can take away from just how far I've come; it's been an extraordinary journey that calls for celebration! My younger self would look at the boss bitch I am today with wonder in her eyes, because past successes should never go unacknowledged nor taken lightly. And as much as I'm learning now with each passing moment, my older self will look back someday and feel the same exact fucking way about who I am right now.

I AM A GODDAMN BONFIRE OF TRUTH

I speak an uncompromising truth—I am full of bold motherfucking dreams, and nothing will stop me from realizing them. Not fear or complacency, not bullshit societal expectations nor oppressive systems that seek to limit my power and potential. My courage is fueled by the raging fire in my belly that refuses to be quenched no matter what stands in its way, and there's an energy inside me strong enough for ten lifetimes worth of ambition, passion, and imagination! So today I choose to live bold as fuck, out loud, as if there were no tomorrow, because time isn't something meant for wasting away on settling for bullshit mediocrity.

I WILL AIM FOR PROGRESS, NOT FUCKING PERFECTION

Today is a good day to be kind to myself, and fuck perfection. I don't need to be perfect; I just need to be my best self. I'm capable of greatness, and I will embrace my mistakes, knowing that they make me who I am. I'm more than my flaws, and I won't let them stop me from getting what I want out of life. I'll be kind to myself, and instead of striving for perfection, I'll strive for progress. I'm worth the effort, and I won't let anyone tell me otherwise. I'm strong, I'm courageous, and I'm a fucking badass.

FUCK YOU, PAY ME

I will no longer settle for even one iota less than I fucking deserve. No more excuses, no more bullshit—just a commitment to stay true and hold myself accountable to my own standards. From this moment forward, I refuse to let heartbreak or disappointments define me, and instead realize that they only serve as a reminder that I am strong enough and capable of far greater things! It's time I stop playing small in this world and high fucking time to take my power back by reclaiming the respect and dignity owed to me all along.

MY LIFE, MY PACE, MY FUCKING CHOICE

Today I will listen to my needs and go unhurriedly at my own pace, no matter what anyone else says. This is an act of self-love that defies the expectations placed on me by the horseshit we call society's standards. In this world hell-bent on overworking us, it can be hard to feel like we have permission for our time off—but goddamnit I do! My value doesn't come from how much work or hustle I put into something; instead it comes from simply being alive and taking care of myself as best as fucking possible.

SNIP-SNIP MOTHERFUCKERS

I have the courage to stand up for myself and cut off those who no longer bring me joy. I'm not afraid of letting go of what doesn't make me happy, even if it's hard or uncomfortable. It takes strength to walk away from something that hurts, but with a little bit of self-love and resilience, nothing can stop me! While others may try their best to hold on to relationships out of fear or obligation—I know when enough is enough. There comes a time in life when you must move on without looking back for your own personal growth.

I WILL LET MYSELF FUCKING REST AND RESET

I'll be damned if I don't give myself a break every once in a while! This world will run you ragged if you let it, so I'm taking back my power and recognizing that I'm allowed to zone out when I need to. Even my bitching, beautiful brain needs a break from time to time, and I'm not afraid to say it. No one can tell me what's best for my well-being, and that includes taking time for myself. So let's make it official: I'm giving myself permission to relax, recharge, and take a fucking breather whenever I need to.

THE BEST DAMN INVESTMENT IS ME

This weekend, I'm going to fucking own my life and make time to do something I love. I'm going to invest in myself, my creativity and interests, and explore new ones as well. I'm going to take some time for me, because I know exactly what I need—and that's some damn self-care and self-discovery. No more putting myself last. No more self-denial. No more fucking delayed satisfaction. This is my life and it's mine to live, and I'm going to fucking enjoy every single second of it!

I'LL GROW WHEREVER THE FUCK I'M PLANTED

I won't let any motherfucker tell me what I can and cannot become. When life throws shit at me, I'll pick up a shovel and plant the seeds of my success with it! The future is mine to shape; it's time for me to get creative with how I envision my own success. It won't be easy, but nothing worth having ever comes without hard work. No matter who questions or doubts my path, no one can stop me from achieving goddamn greatness if that's what I set out to do!

AIN'T NO MOUNTAIN TOO HIGH FOR THIS BOSS BITCH

I am a goddamned force to be reckoned with, and woe be to anyone who doubts that for a single fucking second. There is no challenge too big for me, no mountain too high, no ocean too vast, and I will not let anything stand in my way. I'm fucking unstoppable when it comes to achieving what's important to me; nothing can hold me back from getting shit done and living my life on *my* own terms. When obstacles come up, they don't stop or slow down the badass woman that I am—instead of shrinking away from them, I take charge and tackle every single one head-on until victory is mine! My determination never falters because success starts with *me*.

WAKE UP AND SMELL THE MOTHERFUCKING ROSES

I'm not one to take shit lying down. I am a woman with a fire in my soul and the courage of a lion. I will not be denied my destiny, and I will not back down. I am driven, focused, and sure as fuck capable of achieving my wildest dreams. The seeds of my success lie within me, and I will use them to cultivate the perfect future I envision for myself. I am powerful and unstoppable, and I will not allow anyone or anything to stand in my way. I will take charge of my life and use my inner strength to help the success I am cultivating to grow. Like a rose garden, I deserve to fucking flourish!

ONLY I CAN MOVE THESE FUCKING GOALPOSTS

I claim my fucking goals. I hold great promise and the power to achieve them, no matter what anyone says or thinks of me. No one can take away this awesome potential that burns within me—not even myself! If someone tries to stand in my way, they had better have great fucking health insurance, because nothing will stop me from achieving greatness with every goddamn breath I take. My ambition knows no bounds as long as I'm willing put forth the effort and hard fucking work necessary for success. So here's to embracing all of life's challenges head-on like a boss bitch ready to conquer any obstacle thrown her way!

TO-DO? MORE LIKE TO-DON'T FUCK WITH ME.

I am far more fucking important than my to-do list. Today, I will choose self-care and prioritize my well-being over any extra tasks that don't need immediate attention. In overwhelming moments, I'll take a breath, pause the hustle and bustle of life's demands, recharge myself with mindfulness or whatever nourishes me—and then resume in alignment with what truly matters most: myself! With the overwhelming crush of modern life, we must be unapologetic about setting boundaries between our work obligations and personal needs, because this is how we become worthy of greatness. So fuck society's expectations—know your worth deeply enough to put yourself first!

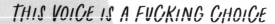

THIS VOICE IS A FUCKING CHOICE

I will not be afraid to speak my damned truth, even if it makes others uncomfortable. I trust in myself and the power of my voice—both literally and figuratively. When times get tough, when challenges arise or shit stands in the way of progress for me and those around me, I can rely on deep reserves within myself that allow me to dig down into a place where courage lives. And at moments like these—as hard as they may be—sometimes walking away is also an act of strength. Trusting what's best for you despite any external pressures or expectations requiring something else from you takes real goddamn grit!

I WILL NOT SELF-EDIT SHIT

I reject the notion that I must police my language in order to be respected. I am not here to tear myself down; I am here to build myself up, and that includes using the words that speak to me and telling the world to go fuck itself whenever I damn well please. I am in charge of my own story, and I will craft that narrative however I fucking choose. I am ready for the next chapter of my life and won't be editing myself down for someone else's taste. I am woman; hear me swear!

NO BOX? NO FUCKING PROBLEM

Fuck thinking outside of the box; it's time for us to take charge of our own lives and think like there is no box! Today and every day, we must trust ourselves enough to believe that we can get out of whatever binds limit us, be it societal expectations or self-doubt. Let's swear off any inner dialogue that diminishes our confidence, in order to create a new narrative—one free from excuses. No more saying, "I'm not ready yet"; let's instead say, "Fuck yeah, I am!" It doesn't matter what anyone else thinks; if you have the will and the skill, then go do it now! Put your game face on and break through those barriers, because one thing is sure as hell true: you got this shit handled!

TREAD CAREFULLY, OR GET SWEPT THE FUCK AWAY!

I swear by my confidence and know that it is always there for me, like an endless raging river coursing through every fucking cell of my beautiful body. It starts at the top of my head and courses down to the bottom of each toe—a never-ending force that can be tapped into whenever I need it most! This strength isn't something bestowed upon or taken away from me; rather, this power rests within me as mine alone to control, and I'll be damned if anyone else tells me how to use *my* power.

GENUINE, 100 PERCENT BADASS

I give myself all the fucking permission in the world to be my authentic self. For not a single damned second will I be ashamed for who and what I am, even if it means facing difficult truths about myself and the world around me. It takes courage to take off the masks we wear; today, I sure as shit choose to have that bravery. Even when things feel uncertain or hard, I can trust in my own power—because no one else has lived this life like me before! Today is an opportunity for growth, a chance for me to show up as unapologetically real without fear of judgment or rejection. Fuck "shoulds" and fuck perfectionism—it's time to accept exactly who I am right now with love and gratitude, so that tomorrow can be even better than today!

I AM A BEACON OF BOSS BITCH ENERGY

I am a radiant force of badassery, and I will not be cowed by anyone's judgment. My worth is inherent and cannot be diminished by criticism or feedback that does not serve me in any way. When given constructive advice with respect, I accept it gratefully as an opportunity to grow. But when faced with jackasses and their useless, disrespectful commentary? Fuck that noise straight to hell. If it doesn't deserve my attention, then it sure as shit won't get it. Instead of getting pulled down into the mire of other peoples' hang-ups, I choose to stay focused on what matters most: cultivating a life rooted in self-love.

FATIGUE IS TEMPORARY. GLORY IS GODDAMN ETERNAL.

I will not be daunted by any fatigue or bullshit uncertainty I am experiencing right now. Instead, I choose to acknowledge and celebrate my accomplishments thus far—no matter how small they may seem in the grand scheme of things. My strength is a source of pride that cannot be diminished nor denied; it's an integral part of who I am and what makes me unique. So fuck anyone who tries to get in my way! Because whatever comes next, it won't stop me from pursuing greatness with every damned fiber of my awesome being.

SNUGGLE UP, BITCHES

I will wrap myself in gratitude like the fuzziest fucking blanket imaginable and let its warmth spread outwards. I am thankful for my strength, my fortitude, my courage—all the traits that make me who I fucking am today. When I'm engulfed by thankfulness, there's an energy radiating from within that comforts me and allows me to share those positive vibes with others around me too. Gratitude is power, and when we take time to appreciate what we have and where life has brought us so far, everything else seems small in comparison. So here's a big hell yes to being grateful for ourselves, our triumphs, and even our worst fucking struggles.

I AM SO FUCKING ENOUGH

I am not just allowed here; I am in fucking charge here. I swear to you, I will no longer allow my self-talk to be negative. I will no longer tear myself down. This is the time to rise, to build each other up, to celebrate ourselves for the astonishing people we are. I am in charge of my own future, and I will not be defined by the negative opinions of others. I'll take ownership of my voice and my worth because that is enough for me. I will make damn sure it's enough for everyone else too.

I AM A MIGHTY FUCKING OAK!

I'm done waiting and doubting myself, and I sure as shit won't let anyone tell me what's possible or impossible anymore—that kind of thinking is bullshit anyway! This moment, right now, everything is as it should be, so fuck fear straight off to where it belongs! Everything I desire will come to pass in its own due time. Instead of worrying about when the changes are going to happen, I'll focus on taking care of myself and trusting my intuition, so that once they do arrive, they can set down roots within a solid foundation. My future isn't predetermined by someone else's standards. It belongs only to me. Everything is happening when it should and as it should.

I'VE FOUND MY FUCKING PEOPLE

I'm fucking loved and I know it. Whenever I feel lonely, I'm reminded of the people who support me, accept me, and make me feel secure and heard. I'm never alone and deserve to be surrounded by the individuals who make me feel like I can do anything. I can do anything I put my mind to, and anyone worth half a shit would be able to see that from a mile away. Luckily, I have those people in my life, and I'm endlessly thankful for those beautiful bastards.

TIME TO CHILL THE FUCK OUT

I will cut myself some slack and take a break from pushing too hard, because I fucking refuse to let social pressures become an impossible burden to bear. Instead, I promise to remember that tomorrow is always another day for growth, reflection, and renewal. Too many of us can often feel like our worthiness must be proved through exhaustive effort or perfectionism—but fuck that! We all deserve grace in the pursuit of self-improvement while still allowing ourselves moments to just chill out without guilt. That doesn't make us any less badass or capable—it makes us better equipped to achieve anything we set our hearts on.

CALL ME DOUBLE-OH-BAD BITCH

I am a goddamn change agent, and I have the power to create positive transformation in my life. I'm done with settling just for what's comfortable, because it sure as shit won't get me where I want or need to go. So here's a hell yes to taking leaps of faith into new opportunities, pushing through self-doubt and fear, and confronting old habits head-on so they can finally be released from their grip over my life trajectory. From this point forward, you can be damned sure that nothing will stop me from becoming who I know deep down inside I was always meant to become: strong, capable, and powerful beyond all imagination.

I WILL PUT MYSELF FIRST, MOTHERFUCKERS

I'm fucking done with putting myself last. Starting from this moment, I will put myself first and take care of myself like I fucking deserve. To hell with anyone who says that self-care and self-love are at all selfish—they are damn essential for my well-being and happiness. I refuse to accept anything less than that for myself. From now on, I'm going to make sure my needs come first, and you can be damned sure that I'm not going to apologize for it.

I AM THE AGENT OF MY OWN FUCKING DESTINY

I am exactly where I need to be right now. And if for any reason, at any time, that doesn't work for me anymore? Fuck it! It's my life, and I'm going to choose the path best suited to what makes sense in each moment. Embracing change is a part of embracing self-empowerment, no matter how hard or uncomfortable it may feel. Every decision we make can bring us closer to our goals with confidence and courage—even when those decisions are difficult ones. No one else can define who you want to become but yourself—so go ahead and redefine your own rules as needed because you have agency over your own journey!

TEST ME AT YOUR OWN FUCKING PERIL, WORLD!

In the face of difficult relationships, I will not be fucking silenced. My feelings are valid, my thoughts matter, and you can be damn sure that I won't back down from standing up for them. When interpersonal situations become stressful, it's okay to feel angry or scared, but no one can take away my right to express myself with clarity and confidence. No more shying away; if something isn't working in a relationship, I'll have the courage to speak out about how damn frustrated I am instead of bottling everything up inside me! To hell with being afraid—when push comes shove (literally!), it's time for me stand firmly on my own two feet—because that is exactly what makes me strong!

I AM OPEN AS HELL TO LEARNING

I choose not to be a victim of circumstance, but rather a badass agent of my own destiny who is capable of withstanding difficult times. Even when it's hard for me to accept, I welcome all things that come into my life, knowing full well there will be some shitstorms along the way that test every ounce of grit inside me. Yet even in those moments, I remember how mighty and brave I am, and that by embracing these challenges I also give myself permission to learn from them. Every experience is a motherfucking teacher.

LIGHT HEART, BAAAAD ASS

I deliberately choose to embrace my inner child, and I don't give a fuck what anyone else thinks about that. Even if it's just for today, I'll put aside all of the pressure that society puts on me to be perfect or successful or mature or composed—none of that matters right now. Instead, I'm going to focus on having fun and being lighthearted with no apologies! Life is too short not to enjoy every moment as they come without worrying about some arbitrary standard set by others. So fuck 'em, this day belongs entirely to me and my wildest dreams!

COMPROMISE + COMPASSION = COMPLETELY FUCKING BADASS

I refuse to listen to bullshit demands that I suppress my voice or what I stand for. That being said, it doesn't mean that compromise isn't an option; it only means that when I do choose to give a little of myself in order to make space for another person's opinion or ideas, fucking hell—it will be because I want to! Compromise is an opportunity to not only practice compassion toward others, but also to remind myself how important self-compassion is, because kindness is one of the most badass things a person can do.

I WILL TAKE ONE DAY AT A DAMN TIME

I am on no one's fucking timeline but my own. I'm too smart and savvy to expect greatness right away, but if and when it comes, I won't be too burned out to recognize or savor the moment. No matter what today brings me— good or bad—tomorrow is always another opportunity for a new beginning. As long as I keep this in mind and focus on making it through each day with grace and courage, I'll have what it takes to keep getting through.

LIFE IS SHORT— AND OH-SO- FUCKING BEAUTIFUL!

Today is a gift, and you can be fucking sure that I'm not going to waste it. Life may be short, but that doesn't mean I can't make the most of it—every second counts! No more waiting around for permission or approval; this moment is mine, and nothing's going to stop me from embracing my destiny. It's time to break through barriers, ignore naysayers, rise above bullshit—because if there's one thing guaranteed in life, it's that we have no fucking clue what tomorrow will bring. So now's the time to take charge and start living unapologetically on our own terms—it sure as hell beats sitting around like an idle motherfucker wasting away another day of possibility.

I AM IRRE-FUCKING-FUTABLE FUCKING PROOF OF EVOLUTION

I will not let anyone define me, restrict me, or limit my immense fucking potential. I am constantly evolving and growing into the person I want to be—and fuck anyone who doesn't believe in that! Every day is another opportunity for self-discovery; every moment a chance to learn more about myself and what makes me powerful. As pieces of my identity shift and change, I have the strength to adapt with grace—letting go of those parts of myself that no longer serve me, while embracing all new aspects as they slot into place. This is how I choose to love myself: fiercely and with zero reservations.

PRESENT? I'M A FUCKING GIFT.

Today, I'm embracing the power of my presence. It's not always easy to stay focused when there are so many distractions around me—but who gives a fuck about easy? Today is about being present with the people in front of me, staying true to myself, and getting shit done without any apologies or excuses. My past and future both play a part in who I am, but today I will allow my strength to come from being present in the moment, from connecting deeply with the world around me, and no amount of bullshit or fuckery can distract me from that.

I WILL STOP FUCKING MASKING

Today I will tap into my true feelings without an ounce of fucking apology. No more pretending to be someone else or glossing over what's real for me. No matter how uncomfortable it may feel, I'm ready to take a closer look at my authentic, bad bitch self and let go of the mask so I can become the person I really want—not just the things that were expected of me by others. Make no mistake: this is an act of motherfucking bravery. Intentionally curating a life that brings out the best in myself, in harmony with my true values, is the most important part of this beautiful, fucked-up thing we call life!

I AM THE MAP TO MY OWN DAMN FUTURE

I will confidently navigate each step of my journey like the badass intrepid explorer I am, no matter how winding the path may be. Even when I cannot see where it is leading me yet, I trust in myself that I have all capabilities to reach clarity and success. My strength lies within me—not others' expectations or approval—so fuck what anyone else has to say about who they think I should be! This is *my* journey; with confidence and courage as my guiding stars, nothing can stop me from reaching the destination of freedom and self-fulfillment on this wild ride we call life.

DO YOU FEEL FUCKIN' LUCKY, PUNK?

I am a loaded fucking weapon of badassery and ability, and nothing will stand in my way. I know who I am—strong, precise, effective—and that knowledge gives me the courage to take risks. No matter what challenges come my way, no matter how hard it gets or how much shit is thrown at me from all sides—I stay true to myself and press forward with grit and determination. Knowing who you are gives you courage, and knowing your worth makes you unstoppable, and that's why "I know myself" will forever remain one of my favorite bad bitch mantras as each day passes by.

READY. SET. SLAY.

I am fucking ready. Ready to take on the world, ready to forge ahead and smash any barrier that stands in my way, ready to be the badass woman I know I'm meant to be. I know that motivation is always within me—all I have to do is say, "I am ready," and believe it with every fiber of my being for it to come quickly and effortlessly. There are no limits when it comes to what's possible when I support myself, and only those imposed by my own fear or doubt can stop me from achieving whatever I set out for.

I GIVE; NOW I SHALL FUCKING RECEIVE

I will allow myself to receive the kindness that I give to others every day, whether from external sources or my own damned self. Far too often we allow ourselves to deny our own worth, but no fucking longer! No more self-criticism and doubt, no more bullshit small talk about how far away success feels. Today is a new day, one where I take care of me first before anyone else—with gentleness, compassion, and love for who I am right now in this moment. Fuck yes, today is my time for freedom and joy!

MY BAD BITCH SENSE IS TINGLING

I am the master of my own choices, and I trust my gut fucking instincts. If something doesn't feel right, then hell no—I won't do it! My body is mine to control, and you can be damned sure that nobody else gets a say in what's best for me. No matter how much pressure someone puts on me or tries to push their agenda on me, at the end of the day I have full agency over myself and make decisions that are authentic to who the fuck I am.

I AM ONE OF A DAMN KIND

No one else can ever be me, and that's fucking amazing. I'm growing every day and becoming a badass. I am so fucking incredible, and don't you dare let your beautiful ass forget it. I can do anything, and I'm doing a phenomenal job. I am powerful and unique, and that in itself is sure as hell something to be proud of. I will embrace my individuality and keep growing and learning. I have something special, and will stay strong and keep being that beautiful bitch we know I am.

ONE BREATH, ONE STEP, ONE BADASS BITCH

I will not apologize for taking up space. For just five minutes, I will walk outside and let the wind kiss my skin and the sun warm my face. I will take a deep breath and be unapologetically me. My body is mine to own—it's part of who I am, an integral piece of my identity that cannot be taken away from me or diminished by anyone else. So fuck what they say; with every step forward, every breath in and out, I'm reclaiming ownership of myself.

NO DOUBT, ALL FUCKING CLOUT

Today I'm not going to be guided by doubt. When my heart is pounding and my stomach feels like it's flipping, I know that means I'm stepping outside of my comfort zone—a place where amazing things happen! There is no halfway for me today; instead, I'll give everything all the fucking way. My courage will carry me through any challenge standing in front of me and make sure nothing can hold me back from what's mine to own. This is how badass women do shit: fearless and unafraid to take risks because we trust ourselves enough knowing there are beautiful rewards waiting on the other side if we're brave enough to go get them!

ADVANTAGE? ME, LOVE.

I will not be taken advantage of any fucking longer, and I am done with being too nice and putting people before me in order to make them happy. From now on, my well-being is going to come first—no ifs, ands, or buts about it! No one can fuck with me anymore. No more letting others take the reins when it comes to what's best for me. This isn't selfishness, it's self-care, and it's an important part of living a fulfilled life that many have forgotten how to practice properly. It doesn't matter who you are—nobody messes with this badass bitch without consequences!

KNEEL, MOTHERFUCKERS. ROYALTY IS PRESENT.

Today I am claiming my throne as the fucking queen I am. I'm done with people, places, and things that leech away the energy to become who I was meant to be. From now on, if something doesn't fucking energize me, then it's not worth making room for! It starts today. When given the choice between draining activities and those that restore my spirit—no fucking doubt about where I'll put my time and attention! Self-care isn't selfish; taking care of myself so that others can benefit too is an act both brave and badass as fuck. Today marks a new era—one filled with lightness instead of dread, possibility rather than obligation, commitment over confusion... The possibilities are endless.

EFFORT IS WHAT MAKES A BADASS. OUTCOME IS SECONDARY.

I'm a fucking badass who won't let the outcome define my worth. Instead I'll celebrate all of the hard work and effort that got me here. Every expert was once a beginner—and that includes me too! With perseverance, strength, and self-love, nothing is out of reach for me to achieve, and beating myself up for what could have been will only fucking hold me back. Instead of focusing on what could have been or should have been done differently in hindsight, I will take pride in how far I've come from where I began. So show me your fucking worst, life; I'm only getting started!

I WON'T FEED MY FUCKING FEARS

My faith in humanity gives me all the damned courage I need to keep going every day, no matter what obstacles stand in my way. And when things get tough? That's all right—I know how to fight for myself and others with all of fucking fury inside me, even if sometimes it means doing something scary or uncomfortable. No matter what happens today or tomorrow, I choose love over fear always, knowing full well that whatever transpires down the line will be met with pride and bravery. I'm going to greet those fears and insecurities as I pass them fucking by, and I won't feed them. I am the fucking champion of my own life, and I choose hope over fear!

MAXIMUM EFFORT, MAXIMUM FUCKING REWARD

I vow not to let anyone or anything stand in the way of me doing what is right for myself and others around me. There are no limitations on who can create change in this amazing dumpster fire known as life. So today, I'm taking charge by using every damn ounce of strength within me as a mighty force for good in this beautiful, fucked-up world. No matter how small it may seem at first glance—each step forward has an impact greater than one could ever imagine—starting with making someone's day just a little bit brighter through positive energy and words of encouragement. Believe you have power? Then you better fucking use it wisely. Go out there and own your unique place in the universe.

I AM MY OWN FUCKING HOME

This fact makes me unbreakable—a fortress of power that no one can breach, a sanctuary with walls of pure fucking steel. So long as I maintain belief in myself and hold strong to my values, nothing and no-fucking-body can stop me from living life on my terms. And for those who dare to try? Prepare for fucking problems, because I will protect my home no matter fucking what. Every day is another chance to build myself up inside out until every corner of this house called "me" exudes beauty and strength like never before!

CALL ME FUCKIN' WONDER WOMAN

My freedom is a superpower, and I will not be shamed for using it. Even when others don't recognize or respect my values, goals, and identity—I fucking hold on to them anyway. It's okay to disagree with people who do not honor me; in fact, standing up for myself shows strength of character that nobody can take away from me! My voice matters just as much as anyone else's, and if they cannot accept the realness that comes along with this, then they can get straight to fucking themselves. They are missing out on something special, but their short-sighted jackassery does nothing to diminish my worthiness. At the end of the day, I am enough— exactly how I am.

OH, CAPTAIN, MY FUCKING CAPTAIN!

I am the master of my own destiny and the captain of my own fucking ship. I will not let anyone or any antiquated rules and norms dictate how I live my life. The world can throw all kinds of bullshit at me, but that won't stop me from doing what brings joy to myself and others no matter if it has a purpose outside itself or not! No one is going to tell me who to be or take away the things I enjoy in this short time we have on earth. So go ahead, dance like nobody's watching, sing your heart out even when you're off-key... Whatever makes *you* happy without hurting yourself or another living being, just do it, because you deserve every damned bit of pleasure there is for simply existing.

EVERY DAY, EVERY CHOICE—
ALL FUCKING MINE

Today I'm reclaiming my motherfucking power and taking control of my life. As a woman, I have the goddamn strength to create an environment that is conducive to my growth and success. With every breath, I remind myself that it's up to me where and how I choose to live each day, and that no one else can decide for me what will make this journey exciting or worthwhile. Today—and every day—I am deciding how things are going down in my world, and if something needs spicing up? Then so fucking be it!

I AM IN A LIFELONG RELATIONSHIP
WITH MY DAMN SELF!

Each day, I am becoming more and more damn sure of who I truly am. Each challenge faced, each loss endured, every success celebrated brings me closer to that single overarching goal. As a woman in this world today, it is so fucking important for me to remember the power within myself, not just on days when things are going right, but especially those times when everything feels wrong. I can stay true to myself through any storm, because at the end of it all there will be growth and lessons learned if I choose to see them as such.

BEING MYSELF? YEAH, I'M A FUCKING EXPERT.

I'm fucking amazing at being me. Like, extraordinarily fucking good. Trying to be someone else only saps my energy and keeps me from showing the world who I really am—the real, unique person that only I can be! My confidence in myself is unshakable; it's what gives life its flavor and makes living an adventure. There will always be naysayers trying to get between me and achieving greatness, but their words won't stop how powerful I truly feel within. No matter where this journey takes me or whatever challenges come up along the way, no one has power over my destiny except for me.

I AM PRESENT, AND SUCCESS IS MY GODDAMN FUTURE

I'm sick and tired of living in the past, worrying about things that I can't control. It's time to take control of my life and live in the here and now, knowing that I'm strong enough to take on whatever comes my way. I'm a badass woman who isn't afraid to face the struggles of today, and I won't let the worries of tomorrow fuck up my present. I'm ready to take on the day and make my life happen, and I won't let anxiety or fear hold me back. I'm here and ready to live now and make it the best it can be.

NO LOOKING BACK, NO HALF MEASURES, TODAY I'M ALL FUCKING IN

I'm done with settling for anything less than the best. No more fucking "good enough" or "it'll do." Yesterday may not have gone as planned, but I refuse to give up on myself and my dreams. Today is a new day full of possibility—one filled with potential that's fucking mine for the taking! No matter what happened yesterday, today will be better because it has to be; there are too many damn opportunities in life waiting to be seized. So here's to declaring that from this moment forward, the best is yet ahead of me—let's motherfucking do this!

THIS AIN'T MY FIRST FUCKING RODEO!

I am a damned creative goddess, and I won't let my thoughts go unheard. My ideas are powerful, unique, and radically honest, bursting from the depths of my being when I allow myself to be vulnerable without fear or judgment. Creative ideas always run through me like wild fucking mustangs over an open prairie; all it takes for them to materialize is for me to let go of the reins and trust in my innate ability to manifest greatness with each thought. So here's some real talk: let go of the reins, and unleash your imagination today, because you can do anything if you just believe in yourself!

MY DECISIONS ARE MINE—
NO MATTER THE DAMN OUTCOME

I am a motherfucking badass and I know it. I'm going to own my flaws, my mistakes, and my bad decisions. No matter how hard I fuck up, I'm still worthy of love and acceptance. I love other flawed people, so I'm going to start by loving my flawed self just as much. I'm going to learn to embrace everything about me, the good and the bad, and be happy with who I am. I'm capable and powerful, and I'm going to show the world just how fucking amazing I am.

I AM SHOCKINGLY FUCKIN' AWESOME

I am a live fucking wire of ability, bursting with untapped potential. I can feel its power coursing through my veins, and it drives me to keep pushing forward into the unknown. By merely setting out to achieve something, no matter how daunting or far-reaching that goal may be, I have already set in motion a powerful force of success. With every step taken on this journey toward greatness comes an even greater sense of confidence within myself, and fuck what anyone else thinks, because they don't know shit about where I'm headed. No one will ever take away my ambition for self-betterment nor dim the light radiating inside these bones. This is my time to shine, and nothing can fuck with that.

I AM JOY. I AM RAGE. I AM MOTHERFUCKING HUMAN.

I grant myself permission to experience the full range of my emotions, from joy to fear to anger to despair. No feeling is too much for me, because they are all part of this messy fucking experience known as being human. To deny them would just be bullshit, not only to myself but also those around me who benefit when I accept these feelings with grace instead of trying to ignore them or escape their clutches. Instead, by staring into the mirror with unflinching badassery, no matter how uncomfortable it may feel, I can learn valuable lessons about life while simultaneously growing into the best damned version of myself possible!

I AM THE SHATTERER OF FUCKING MOLDS!

I will not accept any role that does not fucking fit me like a damned glove. I have a jar of awesomeness brimming with unique talents and skills, so if something doesn't feel right or isn't working out for me, then fuck it! There's no point in wasting my time settling into an uncomfortable mold when I can instead spend time to find the perfect place where I can shine—one made especially for me. The world has too much shit going on already, so why add more by forcing myself on to someone else's timeline? My worth lies in being authentic about who I am: strong-willed, ambitious, powerful as hell, and ready to take chances even if they scare the crap out of me.

I AM MY OWN DAMNED PERMISSION SLIP

I won't wait for permission. I am the one in charge of my life, and I sure as shit will not let anyone else make decisions for me. If I want to change, then it is up to me alone to choose that path and take control over my own destiny. No longer will I sit back, waiting and hoping that someone chooses me. Instead, I'll be the one doing the choosing, and to hell with anyone who thinks they can stop me. If there's something out there worth having or fighting for, then I'll damned sure go get it myself, because nothing can stop an empowered woman from taking the future into her own hands!

BACKSEAT DRIVERS CAN GTFO

Everyone else can keep their hands off the goddamned steering wheel of my life. No more letting other people dictate my choices. No more playing second fiddle when I should be center fucking stage. Life is a series of choices, and I'm determined to make the ones that will bring me happiness and success. I'm taking the power to start down a new path and create the life I want for myself, no matter how difficult it may be. I'm strong and capable, and I'm not afraid to make brave decisions and take bold steps toward my future, no matter what consequences may come.

FILL THAT CUP TO THE FUCKING BRIM!

Today I will take time to prioritize myself. Caring for others is important, but self-care is fucking essential and nonnegotiable. I need to remember that taking care of myself is not selfish; it's fucking necessary. I will choose to take some time to do things that make me feel good and fill my cup. I will be kind to myself and recognize my worth. I will not feel guilty for putting my needs first. By taking care of myself, I can be there for others in a much more meaningful way. I will prioritize myself today, and that is fucking empowering.

I AM FUCKING LIMITLESS

I am as fierce as a damn lioness, and I know that my self-worth is determined by no one but me. No one can decide what I can and cannot do, no one can else can know or set my limits, and only I can push those damn limits when I'm fucking ready. I am unquestionably, unapologetically powerful, and no one should dare try to tell me otherwise. I know I'm not only capable of doing great things but doing them with style and motherfucking grace. My self-worth is something only I can decide, and I've decided that I'm the most valuable thing in my life.

I'M A RUNNER; I'M A FUCKIN' TRACK STAR

Today, I step into the day with a fierce determination to achieve my goals and dreams. No matter what happened yesterday—no matter how daunting it may have seemed at the time—today is an opportunity for me to create something new. Today brings fresh energy and hope, so hell fucking yes I am going to take full advantage of this momentous occasion and leave all hurdles in my dust as I stride toward greatness on my own terms. With every breath that enters these badass lungs of mine, there's nothing but power radiating from within, fueling each leap forward like never before!

THIS CROWN AIN'T MOVING FOR ANYONE'S BULLSHIT

I will keep my head high, proud, and goddamned regal no matter who or what tries to make me feel small. I won't let anyone's bullshit or lack of respect for me pull this crown from my skull, because no one in this entire damned world can take away the power that comes from being a strong, badass woman—no matter how hard they try! I refuse to be silenced or marginalized by those trying to diminish my worth. Instead, I'll fucking stand up even taller and look out over the kingdom I am creating, confident in the knowledge of just how incredible I truly am.

I'M A CHOOSY BITCH—
AND THAT'S AMAZING

I'm done with letting my past dictate who I am or what I can do. It's time to take back control of how my life moves forward. Fuck the idea that because something happened in the past it has any say over me today; every goddamn day is a new opportunity for growth, learning, and transformation! And no matter where I come from or what mistakes have been made before now—none of that shit matters anymore. My future is determined by me and only me. What kind of person will I choose to be? Which paths will lead to success? That's my choice to make, and choosing is the best fucking part of life.

I AM CALM IN THE DAMN CHAOS

I am the motherfucking eye of the storm, calm amidst chaos. No shrieking winds, no fearsome lightning can ever disturb the peace I have made for myself. When faced with adversity, I stay levelheaded knowing that no matter how chaotic things may seem on the outside, a power lies within me capable of weathering any storm. No bullshit or fuckery can take away my inner peace; it's mine alone to cultivate and keep safe from harm. Today I swear by this truth: nothing will ever break down this serenity within, and so long as I have faith, it can never be destroyed!

MY GUT KNOWS WTF IS UP

I won't let anyone's doubts or judgments define who I am or dissuade me. It doesn't fucking matter if they don't understand why; the only thing that matters is that it means something to me, so damn it, this is my life and I'll do as I please! I will listen closely to myself—thoughts and feelings alike—with understanding and compassion. If an impulse arises within me, it does so for a fucking reason, even if nobody understands that reason but me! All that counts is trusting in my own bad bitch self enough to act on those motivations even when others might not agree.

MY FUTURE IS FUCKING BRIGHT

Today is the day I fight for my motherfucking tomorrow with courage and strength. The future belongs to those of us who have the audacity to speak up against systems that try to oppress us or deny our worth, and our collective power can break down barriers, shatter glass ceilings, and open doors we've been told were off-limits! This isn't about being perfect—it's about having the guts to own your truth no matter how hard it might be at times. Together we can create a more equal world where everyone has an opportunity for success regardless of their circumstances or identity markers—so let's fucking do this!

IT'S NONE OF YOUR DAMN BUSINESS

Today, right now, I'm taking back my motherfucking power. No longer will I let fear, doubt, and insecurity dictate how I show up in the world or what kind of life I'm worthy of living. To hell with anyone who tries to knock me down—they don't know shit about what I've done! From this day forward, only one thing matters: that damn voice inside telling me which path is right for *me*. My confidence comes from trusting myself first and foremost—not from seeking approval from others. This is *my* journey, and it's no one else's damn business but mine!

TODAY I WILL BE FUCKING FIERCE

This morning I get to choose how I will feel, what I do, and who I'll be when I walk out the front door. And today, just watch what motherfucking badassery I'm about to unleash onto this world! It's time for me to own my power with fierce conviction, to let everyone know that no matter what anyone says or thinks of me—and you know those jackasses have opinions—at the end of the day, it doesn't fucking matter because only my truth is important! Today is a chance for me shine brighter than ever before and show them all who really runs shit around here: me!

I WILL ENJOY THE SIMPLE SHIT

I do not need to strive for extraordinary things in order to feel satisfied with my life—ordinary moments, experiences, and objects can bring me goddamn joy if I open myself up to them. Today, when the world is bustling around me and demanding more of my attention than it's worth, I'm so fucking grateful that something as simple as a walk can make such an impact on how contented I feel. Tonight, I'll continue this pact and enjoy the simple amazeballs magic of life, be it awe-inspiring moonlight or some wildflowers tucked away somewhere secret, because beauty lies in even the most mundane places!

NO MORE SUFFERING FOR JACKASSES!

Today is the day I take control and promise to never fucking look back. I vow to myself that I will no longer choose what doesn't make me feel good, or what doesn't give me the respect and value I deserve. I'm taking the wheel and making my own goddamn rules. I'm giving a big fuck-you to what anyone else has to say. Instead, I'll be putting myself first, please and thank you oh-so-fucking much. There are no more excuses, no more delays, and no more settling for anything less. It's time to get up, get out, and give myself the love I fucking deserve.

I'M READY FOR WHAT'S FUCKING NEXT

I know that sometimes it feels like the world is against us, but I promise that greatness will come in time. I vow to take it one day at a time, put my head down, and focus on making it through today. Even when shit gets tough, I will fight to stay clearheaded and open to the possibilities of tomorrow. I am committed to nurturing my resilience, even when it feels like there's nothing left in me. I won't let myself get too burned out to recognize the greatness that's waiting for me. Together, we can start a new chapter tomorrow—with our heads held high and our hearts full of hope. Fuck fear—we got this!

MY DRIP IS LEGENDARY, MOTHERFUCKER

I'm done apologizing for who I am. I'm done suppressing my emotions, my passions, and my voice. I'm fucking done. I am an overflowing fucking fountain of self-love, and I'm ready to fight for the things that I deserve in this life. From this point on, I vow to put in the work to infuse that self-love into areas of my life that lack it. It may be hard at times, but I'll be damned before I let anyone get in the way of creating a world that I love living in—even myself.

SOMETIMES YOU CAN'T PLAN BADASSERY

I give myself grace. I don't have to show up perfectly or please anyone else, and just showing up is sure as shit enough. This isn't easy but damn it, I'm doing the best that I can! Sometimes things won't go as planned—life's a bitch like that—but my self-worth will never be determined by how well something goes according to plan anyway. All of this shit is hard, and all of us are struggling in our own way right now, so there should be no shame in taking time for ourselves when we need it most. At the end of day, whether you're winning or losing doesn't change who you really are: an amazing fucking woman with out-fucking-rageous amounts of inner strength.

GIMME SOME GODDAMN SPACE

I am an unrelenting force, unafraid to stand up for myself and my motherfucking boundaries. I refuse to accept anything less than respect from others—no matter how much they think they know me or care about me. My word is solid steel, carrying more weight than any other person's opinion on what I should do with my life. If I need space, whether it be physical or mental distance from someone else's energy, then damn it, that's exactly what I will demand, and the people who truly love and appreciate me won't hesitate to understand why this is necessary in order for them to have the best version of me around them at all times.

MY JOB DOES NOT FUCKING DEFINE ME

I am more than my job. It is only one piece of the multifaceted person that I am, and it does not determine my whole identity. That being said, fuck yes, I do what I do with excellence! My work ethic speaks to how extra-fucking-ordinary I can be when I focus my energy on something meaningful. Every day, no matter where my career takes me or what challenges come up along the way—from boardrooms to factories to kitchens to home—my commitment remains unwavering. Never let anyone dictate your worth based solely upon your profession; you are so much more capable and resilient than any single title could ever fucking express!

A HIGH TIDE RAISES EVERY GODDAMN SHIP

Even though success can often feel like a competition among others around me, I understand that there's more than enough fucking room enough for everyone at the top, and that my progress does not require anyone else's failure. Instead of competing against each other, let us celebrate one another's victories! My strength comes from within myself; recognizing this allows me to revel in both my and others' successes without bullshit like fear of comparison or envy taking over. Life isn't about winning every single time—it's about enjoying your journey along the way—so fuck it all if someone beats you; support them anyhow!

MY PROBLEM?
YOUR FUCKING PROBLEM.

Fuck it, I'm done taking responsibility for anyone else's decisions. Everyone has their own path to tread, and it's not my place to judge that. I'm a good person, and I try to fucking help where I can, but I won't carry the weight of others' problems on my shoulders, no matter how much I want to help. Instead, I'll trust that each person knows what's best for them and that they can find their own way, just like I do every fucking day. I'm here to be a shoulder to cry on, but I'm sure as hell not obligated to solve anyone else's problems.

TWO PUMPS OF BADASSERY, PLEASE.
HOLD THE BULLSHIT.

Today I'm taking on the world with a hot cup of coffee and a whole lot of fucking motivation! I'm ready to tackle whatever life throws at me, and I'm not afraid to drink it all in. When it comes to caffeine or badassery, consider me a bottomless fucking pit. I'm ready to be the baddest bitch around and show them what I'm made of. I'm on top of the things I need to accomplish today, and nothing can stop me now. So bring it on—I'm ready!

RAW, UNFILTERED, STRAIGHT FROM THE FUCKIN' TAP

I am un-fucking-apologetic in my identity, and I can be fiery, passionate, and strong-willed without any fear of judgment or reprisal. Instead, I embrace my imperfections with courage and grace, because they are part of who I am and make me the unique, amazing badass I am! My character is indelible, imbued in every single thing that makes up the real me: a bad bitch capable of great things. So fuck what anyone else thinks—this is *me* unfiltered, undeterred by convention or expectation! Instead of worrying about how others perceive me, I will focus on embracing my most authentic self without an ounce of fucking fear.

FOCUS, FIRE, AND FEROCITY— FUCK YES

Today, I'm going to show up and give my full attention. No more half-assing or phoning it in. Fuck that! My conversations will come straight from the gut, with no holding back or second-guessing myself, no questioning the worth of my input or the value of my time. When I give people the gift of being fully present and listening deeply, it opens us both up to new possibilities—and that's fucking powerful. By connecting genuinely on an emotional level, we can create strong bonds beyond our everyday conversations, which leads me down paths toward even greater growth opportunities for myself and others.

I CAN SMELL BULLSHIT FROM A MILE AWAY

I'm done playing by other people's bullshit rules, and I'm not asking for any damned permission anymore. Instead, I'm trusting my own damn intuition and honoring my own damn gut. It's time to accept the fact that I don't need to make everyone else happy in order to make myself happy. I'm embracing the power of my own decisions and allowing myself to follow my instincts, even if it means saying, "Fuck you," to the haters. Starting now, I'm not afraid of taking risks and getting out of my comfort zone. I will listen to what my heart tells me and trust that it will lead me closer to true joy.

I WILL NOT SHY AWAY FROM BEING HELLA HONEST

Even if it makes others uncomfortable, I will say what needs to be said when it needs to be said—cost be damned. It's okay for people not to understand or agree, because their opinion does not define me or diminish my power. The only thing that can stop me is myself, so I won't let fear of conflict hold me back any longer! Fuck anyone who tries to oppose what is right or true—they don't get to determine how far I go in life.

CEO WITH BAD BITCH ENERGY

Fuck what anyone else thinks—my self-worth is all up to me! I decide who I am, what I can do, and what I'm capable of achieving. I'm the one who will determine my success in life—no one else. So, let me drop this reminder to myself—I'm an absolute fucking boss, and I'm in control of my life and my decisions. No matter what, I know that my self-worth is determined only by me. No matter what anyone else tells me, I'm the one who decides what I can do and no one else. I'm the captain of my own ship, and I know that I can achieve anything I want, no matter what anyone else thinks.

I MAY FUCKING STUMBLE, BUT NEVER FALL!

You can bet your sweet ass that I'm worthy of forgiveness and learning, no matter how many mistakes I make in life. I have the strength to keep pushing forward no matter the circumstances or fuckery around me, and I sure as hell won't let anything hold me back. I'm done beating myself up for the past; instead, I'll take my mistakes in stride and use them as stepping stones to growth. No more self-judgment, no more self-doubt—it's time to be kind to myself and trust that even if I stumble, I can still fucking make it.

WHEN LIFE GIVES ME LEMONS, I'LL MAKE SOME GOOD FUCKING LEMONADE

I'm done apologizing for who I am and where I come from. Life may have thrown some lemons my way, but you can bet your ass that's not going stop me from making a damn good fucking cocktail out of them! My strength is rooted flexibility and adaptability in the face of adversity. So when those obstacles appear before me, whatever form they take, you can be damn sure I'll face them head on with grace and creativity, with zero self-doubt or bullshit second-guessing!

MY CRYSTAL BALL IS MAGICAL AS FUCK

I am unwavering in my vision, uncompromising in my values, and in charge of my own magical fucking destiny. My intentions are crystal fucking clear: I will create the reality that serves me best. It's up to me to set boundaries and speak my truth without fear or hesitation—no matter how uncomfortable it may be for others around me. This is an act of self-love, resilience, and faith in myself as someone who isn't afraid to say, "Fuck yeah," when something feels right! I trust myself enough to take risks for what matters most so that I can live more authentically aligned with my true badass values.

I'M NOT A WORRIER, I'M A DAMN WARRIOR!

I am a fucking fighter, and my power radiates from within—an unshakable force that can't be contained by anyone but me! Fuck fear—no mountain is too high for me to climb; no challenge is too great for me to conquer with grace and ferocity unparalleled by any! My femininity doesn't mean weakness—it means resilience, intelligence, and fierceness all rolled into one unstoppable package. There are battles still left unsung—let us roar out loud until victory has been achieved!

I WILL PROVE MY INSECURITIES WRONG AS FUCK

I will not be held back by my insecurities any longer. I'm done giving into the fear that keeps me from taking risks and going after what I want out of life. No more listening to negative voices telling me that I can't do it or allowing myself to think less of who I am because of fear. Instead, damn it all—today is a new day! Today, without apology or hesitation, I will give myself the chance to prove my insecurities wrong. And if anyone stands against this truth? They'll have hell itself coming for them!

I DO NOT NEED TO BE PRODUCTIVE "ENOUGH" TO FUCKING REST

I've inherently earned the right to relax and rest whenever I damn well need to. It's a job that needs fucking doing, even if it doesn't seem like one at first glance. Taking an hour or two for myself to unplug and recharge is critical in order for me to keep going strong. Despite all of the to-do lists or fucking influencers pushing me to do more, more, more, I'm not letting anyone else tell me how much shit I should accomplish or how much time I need, because this shit is my call alone, and when I take care of myself first, it makes everything better. Resting isn't just about taking breaks from everyday life, it's also about being motherfucking present with yourself so you can show up more amazingly later down the line.

I WILL CREATE MOTHERFUCKING OPPORTUNITY

Every morning, I give myself permission to be a badass. Screw what anyone else thinks—this is my life and it's time for me to own it! Today, I choose courage over fear, strength over weakness, self-love over shame. No more apologizing or putting up with bullshit from others. I was put on this earth to kick ass and take names. In the face of adversity, I will show up ready as fuck to make an impact on the world around me, because that's how badasses do things: they don't wait for opportunity—they create it.

SHARP WIT? NO SHIT.

I'm a fucking powerhouse of intelligence, and I trust my own judgment to make smart, informed decisions in my day-to-day life. Nobody else can walk this path except me, and I'm the one who chooses where I'm headed and how I fucking get there. I have complete faith in myself and my abilities, and I will never let anyone else second-guess my choices or make me doubt myself for even a fucking second. I'm a strong, independent woman who is not afraid to take ownership of her own destiny. I am a badass and I'm going to fucking own it!

LOUD, PROUD, OBSCENITIES ALLOWED

I'll be damned if I let anyone else decide who I am and how I express myself. I am me and I'll be nothing less; not even the Dalai fuckin' Lama could make me say otherwise. I'm not here to apologize for who I am, and I'm sure as fucking hell not going to let anyone else dampen my spirit. I will not quiet down. I will not be silenced. I'm going to be me, unashamed and unafraid, today and tomorrow, and every goddamned day between here and eternity.

AIN'T NO STRINGS ON THIS BAD BITCH!

I am no one's fucking puppet. I am the uncontested queen and CEO of my own future, and I'll be damned if I let anyone else step in and take control. Sometimes making all the decisions means taking the scary plunge, even if it's intimidating, but you can be damn sure that I'm not letting a little fear stop me. My future self is depending on me, and I'm sure as hell not going to disappoint a woman that fucking awesome. I'm strong, capable, and I will not let fear stand in my way!

BRING IT THE FUCK ON

I am secure and capable of making the best out of whatever comes my way. Even through the roughest periods, I will find something to be grateful for each day. No matter what life throws at me—whether it's a kick in the ass or an opportunity that takes me further than before—I will not let my fear of fucking up hold me back. Mistakes are part of life and learning from them is key; they make us stronger individuals who can keep going despite any setbacks!

FUCK BAGGAGE FEES — I'M FLYING LIGHT TODAY!

I am ready to let go of the bullshit and baggage that has been weighing me down. I will no longer carry it around, because it's not serving my highest purpose...and truth be told, it's fucking exhausting! Instead, I choose to focus on what lies ahead for me and the good things that are inevitably coming my way. My faith in myself is strong and unwavering, and I know deep down within every fiber of my being that great opportunities await me with open arms if only I'm willing to accept them. It isn't going to be easy, but hey—nothing worth having ever fucking is.

WHIRLWIND? HOW ABOUT A WHIRL-FUCKIN-WIN!

Today I will be a good fucking friend to myself! No more getting caught up in the whirlwind of others' wants and needs. It's time for me to take care of my own damn self, because no one else is going to do it as well as I can. From now on, when making decisions big or small, I'm going to ask, "What would make me feel empowered?" I am worthy and deserving of freedom from guilt that comes with putting myself first—whether that's by taking a break after work or saying no without explanation. So today—and every day—I give myself a permission slip to love all parts of who I am, and to hell with anyone who tells me otherwise!

HOLY HELL, I'M AWESOME

I know who I am, and that's a regal fucking queen. It's not always easy to keep that vision in mind, but that doesn't mean my strength isn't real. I have faith in my truth, and that faith keeps me moving when nothing else can, no matter how much fuckery the world throws at me! When life gets hard or confusing, I come back to what matters most—knowing that no matter what happens, nothing can take away from my power as a badass woman!

HUGS ARE AWESOME AS FUCK

I choose to embrace my body and the enormous fucking value of physical contact that it can provide. Today, I will hug a family member, friend, or pet—feeling their warmth and weight in my arms. This connection is nourishment for both of our souls. As I let this overwhelming sense of love fill me up with joy, strength and courage will wash over me too. Knowing there are people who accept and support me unconditionally gives me power in ways no one else can take from me. There is goddamn magic in a simple touch, and I will never forget the badass power in simply holding someone you love.

I WILL LET SHIT GO

I have the power to let go when something isn't meant for me or is no longer serving me. When it's time to move on, I know that there is strength in my decision—in knowing when enough is enough and giving myself permission to leave a situation behind without guilt or regret. This takes courage, but damn it if I don't possess an abundance of it! I'm learning how powerful trusting my gut instinct can be, and even though it may be painful at times, there is still an undeniable fucking power in the act of letting go.

BUT DOES IT BRING ME FUCKING JOY?

I refuse to let any jackasses dictate how I should be living my life. Joy and contentment are not a one-size-fits-all kind of deal. They come in many different shapes and sizes, so it's up to me to create the type that works for me. Happiness looks unique for each individual, but no matter what form it takes on or where we find it, nobody has the right to tell us our version isn't good enough. If it doesn't make me fucking happy, I don't need it. I'm fucking empowered by this realization. No more shitty preset definitions of success or joy—from now on, they're defined solely by me!

I AM FLAWED, I AM HUMAN, I AM BAD AS A MOTHERFUCKER!

Today I will embrace my humanness and all the amazing, fucked-up mess that comes with it. Being human is tough but also beautiful—even on days when it feels like shit. From now on, I will take life's challenges head-on with courage and strength in spite of any blemishes along the way, because they make up who I am as an individual. My struggles don't define me—but rather give me perspective to appreciate even more deeply when things are going well! So fuck perfectionism. Today and every day, humbly accept where you're at right now—all your flaws included—because there's something special about just being alive amidst this chaotic bullshit world we live in.

NO SHAME, NO REGRETS, AND NO FUCKING RESTRAINTS!

I will not strive to fit myself into a dumbass box that society has constructed for me. I will not be afraid to be myself, to make my own decisions, and to do the things that bring goddamn joy to my life. Right now, this moment, I vow to never be ashamed of who I am or how I choose to live my life. No matter what, I will remain true to myself and find the courage to follow my own path. I'm done with trying to be what others want me to be! Fuck society's expectations, fuck social media's standards, and fuck the entire world if it doubts me. Today I will boldly go my own way and live my life free and fucking badass!

KEEP YOUR FUCKING OPINIONS — I HAVE PLENTY

I am my own person, and no jackass or hater can ever take that away from me. I will never let anyone else define who I am or tell me what to think of myself. Their opinions are just their own, and they have fuck-all power over mine! No matter how hard people try to knock down my self-esteem with shitty words and unkind behavior, it's up to *me*—not them—whether those things stick around or go fuck off into oblivion where they belong. It doesn't matter if someone disagrees with me. In the end, all that matters is how highly I value myself as a badass woman who knows her worth and isn't afraid of standing tall for herself at any cost.

STORYBOOK ENDING: BADASSERY IMPENDING

I am the author of my own narrative and I refuse to let anyone else determine how it plays out. My story is mine, and no one can take that away from me. This isn't about perfection or being good enough for someone else; this is about owning who the fuck I am, acknowledging what's important to me, standing up for myself, and always making sure my voice gets heard. It doesn't matter if others don't like my plot twist or disagree with where I'm going. This is *my* damn book, and come hell or high water, I won't stop writing until its finished just the way I want it.

IT'S INTENTS THAT MATTER, AND I'M INTENSE AS FUCK

My reality is a reflection of my intentions, so I'm going to swear to myself that I'm going to shine bright as fuck from here on out! I'm going to be so filled with joy that it radiates off me like a goddamn lighthouse over the cold ocean of bullshit. I'm going to have a wonderful day and won't let anyone bring me down. Today, I'll be the fucking lighthouse keeper of cheerfulness and nothing will stand in my way. Bullshiters and naysayers can sit the fuck down, because I'm going to kick ass and take names! Here's to a day that's going to be full of good vibes and happy energy.

FUCK YOUR RULES IF THEY DON'T SERVE ME

I am taking back my power and unleashing the real me with a mixture of strength, beauty, and courage that makes every damned day a joy. No longer do I have to be put into a box or fit into someone else's expectations of who they think I should be—that shit is over! The real me breaks all the rules; she's brilliant and bold with an unshakable confidence that can't be touched by anyone else. As each second passes, my connection with myself is deepening more than ever before. No one will stop me from living out loud and doing things on my own terms, because there isn't a damned thing stronger than a woman in control of herself!

BATTER UP, MOTHERFUCKERS. I'M TAKING THE PLATE.

I am a badass woman who will not allow tiny people and their problems to get in the way of my ambition. I refuse to let anything stand in the goddamned way of what needs to get done today and instead will focus on accomplishing those tasks before taking care of anything else. When life throws me an unexpected curveball or hits me with an impasse, I'm going to have enough self-respect and strength as a powerful female force to remind myself there's always another path forward—no matter how fucking difficult it may seem at first. And keeping going is exactly what I'll do until everything gets accomplished!

IMPRESSED? I SURE AS HELL AM.

I'm not going to apologize for being myself, and I sure as hell won't try to impress anyone but me. Sure, it's easy to get caught up in what others think of you—the opinions, the judgments—but at the end of the day all that matters is how much I believe in my own power and worthiness. And if someone doesn't like who I am? Fuck 'em! That unhappiness comes from caring too much about other people's thoughts instead of valuing your own opinion first. My confidence will never waver, because no one else's words can define or diminish me. The only voice that truly matters is the one in my own fucking head.

SETTING MYSELF UP
FOR SOME DAMNED SUCCESS!

Today I'm taking charge of my life, coming at it with all the swagger and strength that comes from being a bad, bad bitch. Even when times get tough or things seem overwhelming, I'll remind myself why this matters—because working hard now will pay off in spades for me down the line. And so today? Today is no different. I'm tackling the most important to-dos on my list, not because anyone else expects it, but simply because they matter, and investing time into them now means less stress later on. This isn't about what someone else wants; this is about doing right by myself—and fuck me if that doesn't feel awesome!

I AM COMPLETE—
AND COMPLETELY BADASS

I refuse to buy into the horseshit lie that I can't be complete without another person. My worth doesn't need validation from anyone else—it is inherent, and it fucking rocks! I will choose my own path in life, because no one else gets to define who I am or what success looks like for me. All of the love, attention, and care that should have been given to me by now? I never needed it from them, but from me. From this day forward, regardless of any external factors telling me differently, I know that I am enough just as I am— a fierce force with infinite potential ready for anything life throws my way.

MY INNER VOICE IS A BAMF

I will never apologize for following my own badass heart, even when the path is difficult or unclear. My courage to trust myself is unshakable—it's what has gotten me through so much bullshit already! No one can tell me who I should be or how I should live; only by listening closely to that inner voice of mine can I truly find joy and contentment in life. Even though there are times when doubt creeps into my mind, reminding myself that believing in myself is a bad bitch's greatest superpower gives me a surge of energy unlike anything else. Fuck fear-based thinking; if something feels right, then damn it—let's fucking do it!

I'M GOING TO FRANK-LLOYD-LIGHT THIS SHIT UP!

I am the motherfucking architect of my own life. I recognize that this is an act of incredible power and responsibility, so I choose to use it wisely. Every day, I'm building a foundation for success through hard work and dedication. No matter what bullshit comes my way, nothing can take away from my determination or agency. When faced with adversity, I stand up proudly and fight for myself like a fucking champion! And every action—big or small—shapes each moment into something special so long as it aligns with who I truly am at heart.

TAKE IT OR FUCKING LEAVE IT, THESE ARE MY BOUNDARIES!

I will not allow myself to be brought down by jackasses who are trying to fill my head with unhelpful thoughts and ideas. If a person or situation is no longer bringing me joy, then fuck it—I'm walking away! I am the only one in control of how much energy I give out into this world, so if something isn't making me feel empowered and strong, then why the hell should I stay? When people come at me with negativity, instead of getting dragged into their drama, I'll just turn around and go about living life on my own damned terms and embracing all that brings love and light along the way.

I CAN FUCKING FOLLOW THROUGH

I will show up for me and do anything I set my fucking mind to. I stay with projects until they're done, no matter how difficult or long the process may be. Even when shit gets tough and it feels like giving up is easier than soldiering on, I know that in order for me to make an impactful change in this world—for myself and others—it's worth pushing through and following through on whatever shit stands before me. My commitment gives me strength, my dependability gives others peace of mind, and doing what needs to get done makes me the badass that I am!

PAIN CAN MEAN GROWTH, AND GROWTH IS BADASS

I'm done with being small and playing it safe. I am ready to take up space in this world, no matter what anyone else has to say about it! I will make mistakes along the way—but that's part of growing into my most spectacular self. Fuck expectations, fuck people pleasing or overthinking things because they don't fit a mold set out by someone else. It's taken me years to become who I was meant to be—and goddamnit if I haven't earned every single beautiful, painful moment of growth! My road may have been longer than some—yet here stands an even more powerful version of myself for having gone through these trials and tribulations.

I'M FUCKING GRATEFUL FOR THE SKIN I'M IN

My body is a badass, and it has been there every step along the way: lifting me back up after failure, helping me make hard decisions, pushing through pain so that I can keep going even when it's difficult. It's time to recognize its strength as my strongest ally in this whole damned world. With every breath, I affirm this power. With every morning I wake and open my gorgeous fucking eyes to the world, I will remember to be grateful to this body of mine and all it does for me.

MY LOVE IS BADASS AND FREE — BUT ONLY TO THOSE WORTHY

I am a confident, self-assured woman capable of giving to others without expecting anything in return, and you can bet your ass that I will make sure the relationships I have with myself, my friends, and my family are based on transformative love, not transactional bullshit. My ability to give is rooted in self-respect and respect for those around me, and it's an asset to be used often. I'm aware when someone attempts to take from me more than they're willing to put into our relationship or use manipulative tactics disguised as love. No more bullshit transactions— only real shit: honest conversations about what each person needs and wants out of this connection so we can both truly benefit.